LOVE

90 DEVOTIONS FROM
OUR DAILY BREAD

COMPILED BY DAVE BRANON

Discovery House®
from Our Daily Bread Ministries

Discovery House is affiliated with Our Daily Bread Ministries,
Grand Rapids, Michigan.

Requests for permission to quote from this book should be directed to:
Permissions Department, Discovery House, P.O. Box 3566, Grand
Rapids, MI 49501, or contact us by e-mail at permissionsdept@dhp.org.

ISBN: 978-1-62707-658-6

Printed in the United States of America

First printing in 2016

CONTENTS

FOREWORD

What if someone were to ask you to write down all the things you love—and then to put them in order?

Think of all the possibilities you could choose from: Spouse. Chocolate. Your dog. Church. Pinterest. Friends. Learning things. Babies. Cash. Twitter. Basketball. Grandma and Grandpa. The beach. The Bible. Cat videos. Your hometown. QVC. A perfect pillow. Your smartphone. Ice cream. School. Music. Honesty. Flowers. Yourself. ESPN. A kind word or a smile. Mom. Baby animals. Bacon. Football. God. Shopping. Mountains. Old movies. Starbucks. Sci-fi. New movies. Instagram. Pandas. Nice clothes. Traveling. Camping. Boyfriend or girlfriend. Jesus. The Weather Channel. Fireworks. Pizza. Steph Curry. Your truck. *Dancing with the Stars*. Horses. Facebook. Lists.

In reality, the list is endless. Our world is filled with so many amazing things that capture our attention—things we grow to love because they make us happy or satisfied or fulfilled.

When we look at the list above or at our own personal list of things we love, two entries should stand out. Jesus pinpointed the Top Two Things to Love in response to a question asked by the Pharisees, a religious group that followed Jesus throughout His ministry trying to trip Him up with what they thought were hard questions. They sought to make Him say something that they could use to take Him down.

But when they asked Jesus, "Which is the greatest commandment in the Law?" He responded with an answer that still reverberates across the ages to us with both its simplicity and its clarity. Jesus said, " 'Love the Lord your God with all your heart and with all your soul and with all your mind.' This is the first and greatest commandment. And the second is like it: 'Love your neighbor as yourself' " (Matthew 22:36–39).

So there it is. For all of us who claim Jesus as our Savior and God as our Father, this is the starter kit for our list of things we love. That's because, as Jesus further explained, "All the Law and the Prophets hang on these two commandments" (v. 40). Our understanding of Scripture's teachings are inextricably tied to these two loves. If we love God unconditionally and if we love our neighbors as much as we love ourselves, we can follow through with what God asks us to do in His Word.

Our love of God, along with our love of everyone we come in contact with, is the engine that should drive our interaction with everything else in that list above—or in any list we create.

With that concept of love and its importance in mind, we can turn to the pages of this book and read with new understanding the role of love in our lives. Each of these articles addresses the idea of love based on biblical teaching, and each devotional challenges us in a new way to make godly love the focus of our lives.

We pray that as you make your way through these pages, you'll feel the love—and you'll be challenged to be the kind of person Jesus was talking about when He told His disciples, "By this everyone will know that you are my disciples, if you love one another" (John 13:35).

—*Dave Branon*
Our Daily Bread writer

SELFLESS LOVE

Read: Philippians 2:20-30

[Epaphroditus] almost died for the work of Christ. He risked his life to make up for the help you yourselves could not give me.
—PHILIPPIANS 2:30

While serving in Iraq, a nineteen-year-old soldier saw a grenade being thrown from a rooftop. Manning the machine gun in the turret of his Humvee, he tried to deflect the explosive—but it fell inside his vehicle. He had time to jump to safety. Instead, he threw his body over the grenade in a stunningly selfless act that saved the lives of four fellow soldiers.

This almost unexplainable act of self-sacrifice may help us understand why the Bible tells us that there is a kind of love that is more honorable than having great knowledge or faith (1 Corinthians 13:1–3).

This kind of love can be hard to find—leading the apostle Paul to lament that more people care for themselves than for the interests of Christ (Philippians 2:20–21). That's why he was so grateful for Epaphroditus, a co-worker who "almost died for the work of Christ. He risked his life" in order to serve others (v. 30).

If we think we could never put our own life on the line for others, Epaphroditus shows us the first step with his selfless example. Such love is neither normal nor common, but it doesn't come from us anyway. It comes from the Spirit of God, who can give us the desire and ability to feel for others some of the inexpressible affection God has for us.

—*Mart DeHaan*

No human mind has conceived the things God has prepared for those who love him. 1 Corinthians 2:9

LOVE COMES FIRST

Read: 1 John 4:7-19

We love because [God] first loved us. —1 JOHN 4:19

One evening my friend showed me one of the three decorative plaques that would be part of a wall arrangement she was installing in her living room. "See, I've already got *Love*," she said, holding up the plaque with that word written on it. "*Faith* and *Hope* are on order."

So, Love comes first, I thought. *Faith and Hope soon follow!*

Love *did* come first. In fact, it originated with God. First John 4:19 reminds us that "we love because [God] first loved us." God's love, described in 1 Corinthians 13 (known as the "love chapter"), explains a characteristic of real love when it says, "Love never fails" (v. 8).

Faith and hope are essential to the believer. It is only because we are justified by *faith* that "we have peace with God through our Lord Jesus Christ" (Romans 5:1). And *hope* is described in Hebrews 6 as "an anchor for the soul, firm and secure" (v. 19).

One day we will no longer need faith and hope. Faith will be exchanged for the reality of being with Jesus, and our hope will be realized when we see our Savior face to face. But love is eternal, for love is *of* God and God *is* love (1 John 4:7–8). "Now these three remain: faith, hope and love. But the greatest of these is love"—it is first and last (1 Corinthians 13:13).

—*Cindy Hess Kasper*

Love is not proud. 1 Corinthians 13:4

WHO IS MY NEIGHBOR?

Read: Luke 10:30-37

The expert in the law replied, "The one who had mercy on him."
Jesus told him, "Go and do likewise." —LUKE 10:37

Mary enjoyed her midweek church group meeting as she and several friends gathered to pray, worship, and discuss questions from the previous week's sermon. This morning they were going to talk about the difference between "going" to church and "being" the church in a hurting world. She was looking forward to seeing her friends and having a lively discussion.

As she picked up her car keys, the doorbell rang. "I'm so sorry to bother you," said her neighbor, Sue, "but are you free this morning?" Mary was about to say that she was going out when Sue continued, "I have to take my car to the repair shop. Normally I would walk or cycle home, but I've hurt my back and can't do either at the moment." Mary hesitated for a heartbeat and then smiled. "Of course," she said.

Mary knew her neighbor only by sight. But as she drove her home, she learned about Sue's husband's battle with dementia and the utter exhaustion that being a caregiver can bring with it. She listened, sympathized, and promised to pray. She offered to help in any way she could.

Mary didn't get to church that morning to talk about sharing her faith. Instead, she gave a little bit of Jesus's love to her neighbor who was in a difficult situation.

—*Marion Stroud*

___

Love does not dishonor others. 1 Corinthians 13:5

FRESH MERCIES

Read: Lamentations 3:21–26

Because your love is better than life, my lips will glorify you.
—PSALM 63:3

On a recent airline flight the landing was a little rough, jostling us left and right as we went down the runway. Some of the passengers were visibly nervous, but the tension broke when two little girls sitting behind me cheered, "Yeah! Let's do that again!"

Children are open to new adventures and see life with humble, wide-eyed wonder. Perhaps this is part of what Jesus had in mind when He said that we have to "receive the kingdom of God like a little child" (Mark 10:15).

Life has its challenges and heartaches. Few knew this better than Jeremiah, who is also called "the weeping prophet." But in the middle of Jeremiah's troubles, God encouraged him with an amazing truth: "The faithful love of the LORD never ends! His mercies never cease. Great is his faithfulness; his mercies begin afresh each morning" (Lamentations 3:22–23 NLT).

God's fresh mercies can break into our lives at any moment. They are always there, and we see them when we live with childlike expectation—watching and waiting for what He alone can do. Jeremiah knew that God's goodness is not defined only by our immediate circumstances and that His faithfulness is greater than life's rough places. Look for God's fresh mercies today.

—*James Banks*

Love is patient.

1 Corinthians 13:4

ж

UNSEEN, YET LOVED

Read: 1 Peter 1:1-9

Though you have not seen him, you love him; and even though you do not see him now, you believe in him and are filled with an inexpressible and glorious joy. —1 PETER 1:8

Like others in the blogging community, I had never met the man known to us as BruceC. Yet when his wife posted a note to the group to let us know that her husband had died, a string of responses from distant places showed we all knew we had lost a friend.

BruceC had often opened his heart to us. He talked freely about his concern for others and what was important to him. Many of us felt like we knew him. We would miss the gentle wisdom that came from his years in law enforcement and his faith in Christ.

In recalling our online conversations with BruceC, I gained a renewed appreciation for words written by a first-century witness of Jesus. In the first New Testament letter the apostle Peter wrote, he addressed readers scattered throughout the Roman Empire: "Though you have not seen [Christ], you love him" (1 Peter 1:8).

Peter, as a personal friend of Jesus, was writing to people who had only heard about the One who had given them reason for so much hope in the middle of their troubles. Yet, as a part of the larger community of believers, they loved Jesus. They knew that at the price of His own life, He had brought them into the everlasting family of God.

—*Mart DeHaan*

———

Love does not envy. 1 Corinthians 13:4

START WITH ME

Not looking to your own interests but each of you to the interests of the others. —PHILIPPIANS 2:4

I call them Mell Notes—little comments my daughter Melissa made in her Bible to help her apply specific passages to her life.

In Matthew 7, for instance, she had drawn a box around verses 1 and 2 that talk about not judging others because, when you do, "with the measure you use, it will be measured to you." Next to it she wrote this Mell Note: "Look at what you are doing before you look at others."

Melissa was an "others-oriented" teen. She lived the words of Philippians 2:4. Her classmate Matt, who knew her from church nursery through her final days in the eleventh grade when she died in a car accident, wrote of Melissa in a memory book: "I don't think I ever saw you without a smile or something that brightened up people's days." Her friend Tara wrote this: "Thanks for being my friend, even when no one else was as nice and cheerful as you."

In a day in which harsh judgment of others seems to be the rule, it's good to remember that love starts with us. The words of Paul come to mind: "Now these three remain: faith, hope and love. But the greatest of these is love" (1 Corinthians 13:13).

What a difference we'll make when we look at others and say, "Love starts with me." That's a perfect reflection of God's love for us.

—Dave Branon

Love keeps no record of wrongs. 1 Corinthians 13:5

LOVED TO LOVE

Read: Deuteronomy 10:12–22

And you are to love those who are foreigners, for you yourselves were foreigners in Egypt. —DEUTERONOMY 10:19

The life of pastor Dietrich Bonhoeffer was at risk every day he remained in Hitler's Germany, but he stayed anyway. I imagine he shared the apostle Paul's view that being in heaven was his heart's desire, but staying where he was needed was God's present purpose (Philippians 1:21). So stay he did!

As a pastor he offered clandestine worship services and resisted the evil regime under Hitler.

Despite the daily danger, Bonhoeffer penned *Life Together*—a book on hospitality as ministry. He put this principle to the test when he lived and worked in a monastic community and when he was imprisoned. Every meal, every task, and every conversation, Bonhoeffer taught, was an opportunity to show Christ to others, even under great stress or strain.

We read in Deuteronomy that in the same way God ministered to the Israelites who were leaving Egypt, He instructed them to imitate Him by loving and hosting strangers and widows (10:18–19; Exodus 22:21–22). Likewise, we are loved by God and empowered by His Spirit to serve others in countless ways each day through kind words and actions.

Who on our daily journey seems lonely or lost? We can trust the Lord to enable us to offer them hope and compassion as we live and labor together for Him.

—*Randy Kilgore*

Let love and faithfulness never leave you. Proverbs 3:3

WATER, HOPE, AND GOD'S LOVE

Read: Psalm 112

Even in darkness light dawns for the upright,
for those who are gracious and compassionate and righteous.
—PSALM 112:4

In the African country where my friend Roxanne serves others, water is a precious commodity. People often have to travel long distances to collect water from small, contaminated creeks—leading to sickness and death. Because of the lack of water, it is difficult for organizations like orphanages and churches to serve the people. But that's beginning to change.

Through Roxanne's leadership and the unselfish gifts of some loving people in established churches, clean water wells are being dug. At least six new wells are now operational, allowing churches to be centers of hope and encouragement for their communities. A health center and a home for 700 orphans will also be opened because of access to water.

This is the kind of love that can flow from believers in Christ because we have experienced the love and generosity of God. Paul says in 1 Corinthians 13 that if we don't have love, our voices clang on people's ears and our faith means nothing. And the apostle John says that if we have material possessions, see others in need, and take action, that's evidence that God's love is abiding in us (1 John 3:16).

God desires that we deal "graciously" (Psalm 112:5 NKJV) with those in need, because His heart is gracious toward us.

—*Dave Branon*

Put on love. Colossians 3:14

LIMITLESS

Read: Psalm 36

Your love, LORD, reaches to the heavens,
your faithfulness to the skies. —PSALM 36:5

Recently, a friend sent me the history of a hymn that I often heard in church when I was a boy:

Could we with ink the ocean fill,
And were the skies of parchment made,
Were every stalk on earth a quill,
And every man a scribe by trade;
To write the love of God above
Would drain the ocean dry;
Nor could the scroll contain the whole
Though stretched from sky to sky.

My friend's note said that these words are part of an ancient Jewish poem and were once found on the wall of a patient's room in psychiatric hospital.

Frederick M. Lehman was so moved by the poem that he desired to expand on it. In 1917, while seated on a lemon box during his lunch break from his job as a laborer, he added the words of the first two stanzas and the chorus, completing the song "The Love of God."

The psalmist describes the comforting assurance of God's love in Psalm 36: "Your love, LORD, reaches to the heavens" (v. 5). Regardless of the circumstances of life—whether in a moment of sanity in a mind otherwise muddled with confusion or during a dark time of trial—God's limitless love is a beacon of hope. It is our ever-present, inexhaustible source of strength and confidence.

—*Joe Stowell*

Love never fails.

1 Corinthians 13:8

TRUE LOVE

Read: John 15:9-17

My command is this: Love each other as I have loved you.
—JOHN 15:12

During the rehearsal for my brother's wedding ceremony, my husband snapped a picture of the bride and groom as they faced each other in front of the pastor. When we looked at the photograph later, we noticed that the camera's flash had illuminated a metal cross in the background, which appeared as a glowing image above the couple.

The photograph reminded me that marriage is a picture of Christ's love for the church as shown on the cross. When the Bible instructs husbands to love their wives (Ephesians 5:25), God compares that kind of faithful, selfless affection to Christ's love for His followers. Because Jesus sacrificed His life for the sake of love, we are all to love each other (1 John 4:10–11). He died in our place so our sin would not keep us separate from God for eternity. He lived out His words to the disciples: "Greater love has no one than this: to lay down one's life for one's friends" (John 15:13).

Many of us suffer from the pain of abandonment, rejection, and betrayal. Despite all of this, through Christ we can understand the sacrificial, compassionate, and enduring nature of true love. You are loved by God! Jesus said so at the cross.

—*Jennifer Benson Schuldt*

God is love. 1 John 4:16

EVEN HER?

Read: Joshua 2:1-14

Was not even Rahab the prostitute considered righteous for what she did when she gave lodging to the spies and sent them off in a different direction? —JAMES 2:25

Imagine looking through your family tree and finding this description of your ancestor: "A prostitute, she harbored enemies of the government in her house. When she was confronted by the authorities, she lied about it."

What would you do about her? Hide her story from anyone inquiring about your family? Or spotlight and praise her in the legends of your family's story?

Meet Rahab. If what we read about her in Joshua 2 were all we knew, we might lump her in with all of the other renegades and bad examples in the Bible. But her story doesn't stop there. Matthew 1:5–6 reveals that she was King David's great-great grandmother—and that she was in the lineage of our Savior, Jesus. And there's more. Hebrews 11:31 names Rahab as a woman of faith who was saved from the fall of Jericho (see Joshua 6:17). And in James 2:25, her works of rescue were given as evidence of her righteous faith.

God's love is amazing that way. He can take people with a bad reputation, transform their lives, and turn them into examples of His love and forgiveness. If you think you're too bad to be forgiven or if you know someone else who feels that way, read about Rahab and rejoice. If God can turn her into a beacon of righteousness, there's hope for all of us.

—*Dave Branon*

We love because [God] first loved us. 1 John 4:19

LOVE WE CAN TRUST

Read: Lamentations 3:13–26

Because of the LORD's great love we are not consumed,
for his compassions never fail. —LAMENTATIONS 3:22

Perhaps the most painful statement a person can hear is, "I don't love you anymore." Those words end relationships, break hearts, and shatter dreams. Often, people who have been betrayed guard themselves against future pain by deciding not to trust anyone's love again. That settled conviction might even include the love of God.

The remarkable thing about God's love for us, though, is His promise that it will never end. The prophet Jeremiah experienced devastating circumstances that left him emotionally depleted (Lamentations 3:13–20). His own people rejected his repeated calls to respond to God's love and follow Him. At a low point, Jeremiah said, "My strength and my hope have perished from the LORD" (v. 18 NKJV).

Yet, in his darkest hour Jeremiah considered God's unfailing love and wrote, "Because of the LORD's great love we are not consumed, for his compassions never fail. They are new every morning; great is your faithfulness. I say to myself, 'The LORD is my portion; therefore, I will wait for him!'" (Lamentations 3:22–24). A person may vow to love us forever yet fail to keep that promise; however, God's love remains steadfast and sure. "The LORD your God goes with you; he will never leave you nor forsake you" (Deuteronomy 31:6). That's a love we can trust.

—*David McCasland*

***

Love must be sincere. Romans 12:9

HE NEVER STOPS

Read: Hosea 10:9-15

Sow righteousness for yourselves, reap the fruit of unfailing love, . . .
for it is time to seek the LORD. —HOSEA 10:12

The Old Testament book of Hosea is the story of God's faithful love for His unfaithful people. In what seems strange to us, the Lord commanded Hosea to marry a woman who would break her marriage vows and bring grief to him (Hosea 1:2–3). After she deserted Hosea for other men, the Lord told him to take her back—to "love her as the LORD loves the Israelites, though they turn to other gods" (3:1).

Later, Hosea was called upon to tell the Israelites that because of their rebellion against the Lord, they would be carried away into captivity by a foreign power. "The roar of battle will rise against your people, so that all your fortresses will be devastated" (10:14).

Yet in the midst of the Israelites' sin and punishment, the grace of God toward His people was never exhausted. In a grace-filled exhortation, He said: "Sow righteousness for yourselves, reap the fruit of unfailing love, and break up your unplowed ground; for it is time to seek the LORD, until he comes and showers his righteousness on you" (10:12).

Even when we have "planted wickedness" and "reaped evil" (10:13), God never stops loving us. Whatever our situation today, we can turn to the Lord and find forgiveness to make a new start. His love never fails!

—*David McCasland*

If I have a faith that can move mountains but do not have love, I am nothing. 1 Corinthians 13:2

A BRIEF MESSAGE

Read: Psalm 117

For great is his love toward us, and the faithfulness of the LORD endures forever. Praise the LORD. —PSALM 117:2

I counted once and discovered that Abraham Lincoln's Gettysburg Address contains fewer than three hundred words. This means, among other things, that words don't have to be many to be memorable.

That's one reason I like Psalm 117. Brevity is its hallmark. The psalmist said all he had to say in thirty words (actually just seventeen words in the Hebrew text).

"Praise the LORD, all you nations; extol him, all you peoples. For great is his love toward us, and the faithfulness of the LORD endures forever. Praise the LORD."

Ah, that's the good news! Contained in this hallelujah psalm is a message to all nations of the world that God's "great love"—His covenant love—is "great . . . toward us" (v. 2).

Think about what God's love means. God loved us before we were born; He will love us after we die. Not one thing can separate us from the love of God that is in Jesus our Lord (Romans 8:39). His heart is an inexhaustible and irrepressible fountain of love!

As I read this brief psalm of praise to God, I can think of no greater encouragement for our journey than its reminder of God's great love. Praise the Lord!

—*David Roper*

A friend loves at all times, and a brother is born for a time of adversity.

Proverbs 17:17

⚹

ROOTED LOVE

Read: Hebrews 13:15-25

Do not forget to do good and to share with others, for with such sacrifices God is pleased. —HEBREWS 13:16

When I think of all the wonders of God's magnificent creation, I am especially awed by the giant Sequoia tree. These amazing behemoths of the forest can grow to around three hundred feet tall with a diameter that exceeds forty feet. They can live more than three thousand years and are even fire resistant. In fact, forest fires pop the sequoia cones open, distributing their seeds on the forest floor that has been fertilized by the ashes. Perhaps the most amazing fact is that these trees can grow in just three feet of soil and withstand high winds. Their strength lies in the fact that their roots intertwine with other Sequoias, providing mutual strength and shared resources.

God's plan for us is like that. Our ability to stand tall in spite of the buffeting winds of life is directly related to the love and support we receive from God and one another. And then, as the writer of Hebrews says, we are to "do good and to share" (13:16). Think of how tough it would be to withstand adversity if others were not sharing the roots of their strength with us.

There is great power in the entwining gifts of encouraging words, interceding prayers, weeping together, holding each other, and sometimes just sitting with one another and sharing the presence of our love.

—*Joe Stowell*

Be rooted and established in love. Ephesians 3:17

LOVE WILL FIND A WAY

Read: 1 Corinthians 13:4-13

Love never fails. But where there are prophecies, they will cease;
where there are tongues, they will be stilled; where there is knowledge,
it will pass away. —1 CORINTHIANS 13:8

Years ago I saw a cartoon that depicted a sour, disgruntled, elderly gentleman standing in rumpled pajamas and robe at his apartment door. He had just secured the door for the night with four locks, two deadbolts, and a chain latch. Later he noticed a small white envelope stuck beneath the door. On the envelope was a large sticker in the shape of a heart. It was a valentine. Love had found a way.

Only love can change a person's heart. The Russian author Dostoevsky, in his book *The Brothers Karamazov*, tells the story of a hardened cynic, Ivan, and his resistance to the love of God. On one occasion his brother Alyosha, a man of deep faith who was confounded by his brother's resistance, leans over and kisses Ivan. This simple act of love burned into Ivan's heart.

Perhaps you have a friend who is resisting God's love. Show His love to that friend, just as God showed love to us when He brought salvation into the world through Jesus. Shower upon others the kind of love described in 1 Corinthians 13—a love that is patient, kind, humble, and unselfish.

Authentic love is a gift from God that we can keep on giving.
—*David Roper*

Love covers over a multitude of sins. 1 Peter 4:8

SIGN LANGUAGE

Read: John 1:14-18

May the Lord make your love increase and overflow for each other
and for everyone else, just as ours does for you.
—1 THESSALONIANS 3:12

A friend of mine pastors a church in a small mountain community not far from Boise, Idaho. The community is nestled in a wooded valley through which a pleasant little stream meanders. Behind the church and alongside the stream is a grove of willows, a length of grass, and a sandy beach. It's an idyllic spot that has long been a place where members of the community gather to picnic.

One day, a man in the congregation expressed concern over the legal implications of "outsiders" using the property. "If someone is injured," he said, "the church might be sued." Though the elders were reluctant to take any action, the man convinced them that they should post a sign on the site informing visitors that this was private property. So the pastor posted a sign. It read: "Warning! Anyone using this beach may, at any moment, be surrounded by people who love you." I read his sign the week after he put it up and was charmed. "Exactly," I thought. "Once again grace has triumphed over law!"

This love for one's neighbor springs from God's kindness, forbearance, and patience with us. It's not the law, but the goodness of God that draws men and women to repentance (Romans 2:4) and to saving faith in His Son Jesus Christ.

—*David Roper*

If we love one another, God lives in us. 1 John 4:12

WHAT LOVE IS

Read: Romans 5:1-8

God demonstrates his own love for us in this:
While we were still sinners, Christ died for us. —ROMANS 5:8

Years ago I asked a young man who was engaged to be married, "How do you know you love her?" It was a loaded question, intended to help him look at his heart's motives for the upcoming marriage. After several thoughtful moments, he responded, "I know I love her because I want to spend the rest of my life making her happy."

We discussed what that meant—and the price tag attached to the selflessness of constantly seeking the best for the other person, rather than putting ourselves first. Real love has a lot to do with sacrifice.

That idea is in line with the wisdom of the Bible. In the Scriptures there are several Greek words for *love*, but the highest form is *agape*—"love that is defined and driven by self-sacrifice." Nowhere is this more true than in the love our heavenly Father has shown us in Christ. We are deeply valued by Him. Paul stated, "God demonstrates his own love for us in this: While we were still sinners, Christ died for us" (Romans 5:8).

If sacrifice is the true measure of love, there could be no more precious gift than Jesus: "For God so loved the world that he gave his one and only Son" (John 3:16).

—*Bill Crowder*

We know and rely on the love God has for us. 1 John 4:16

HOW TO TURN HATE
INTO LOVE

Read: Matthew 5:43-48

Hatred stirs up conflict, but love covers over all wrongs.
—PROVERBS 10:12

The message of Jesus is simple yet astounding: Love your enemies. Do good to those who mistreat you. Repay evil with kindness. When a Christian lives by these principles, he will keep his heart free of hatred no matter how others feel toward him.

Steve Estes reported a remarkable example of this in his book *Called to Die.* In January 1981, Colombian rebels kidnapped Wycliffe Bible translator Chet Bitterman, shot him, and left his body in a hijacked bus. Imagine how his parents and loved ones must have felt at the senseless death of this young man!

But in April 1982, as a demonstration of international good will, the churches and civic groups of Bitterman's native area, Lancaster County, Pennsylvania, gave an ambulance to the State of Meta in Colombia, where the young linguist was killed.

Bitterman's parents traveled to Colombia for the presentation of the ambulance. At the ceremony his mother explained, "We are able to do this because God has taken the hatred from our hearts."

This is the power of Christ in action! When we are wronged and ill will begins turning to hatred in our hearts, we need to ask God to change us and enable us to show kindness to the one who has wronged us. This is the way to turn hatred into love.

—*David Egner*

I love the LORD, for he heard my voice;

he heard my cry for mercy.

Psalm 116:1

⋊⋉

LOVE NEVER FAILS

Read: 1 Corinthians 13

These three remain: faith, hope and love. But the greatest of these is love.
—1 CORINTHIANS 13:13

Poet Archibald MacLeish says that "love, like light, grows dearer toward the dark." This is what he calls the "late, last wisdom of the afternoon." The same is true of our love for one another; it can indeed grow dearer as we age. I have seen it myself in two elderly friends.

Married for over fifty years, Claude and Barbara are still very much in love. One is dying of pancreatic cancer; the other is dying of Parkinson's disease. While visiting them, I saw Barbara lean over Claude's bed, kiss him, and whisper, "I love you." Claude replied, "You're beautiful."

I thought of couples who have given up on their marriages, who are unwilling to endure through better or worse, sickness or health, poverty or wealth, and I am saddened for them. They will miss the kind of love my friends enjoy in their latter years.

I have watched Claude and Barbara over the years, and I know that deep faith in God, lifelong commitment, loyalty, and self-denying love are the dominant themes of their marriage. They have taught me that true love never gives up; it "never fails." Theirs is the "late, last wisdom of the afternoon," and it will continue to the end. May we express that same unfailing love to those who love us.

—*David Roper*

———

Many waters cannot quench love. Song of Solomon 8:6-7

SERVING TOGETHER

Read: Galatians 5:13–16

You, my brothers and sisters, were called to be free. But do not use your freedom to indulge the flesh; rather, serve one another humbly in love.
—GALATIANS 5:13

When Cristine Bouwkamp and Kyle Kramer got married in the spring of 2007, they did something most of us wouldn't think of doing. Instead of hosting a "sit-down dinner," they held a simple reception at the church and invited their guests to help distribute food to people in need.

They bought a truckload of food and had it delivered to the church parking lot. Then they and their wedding guests served the people of the neighborhood. Cristine and Kyle said the first thing they wished to do as a married couple was to serve others. Because God had changed their lives so radically, they wanted to "bless God for blessing us with each other."

The Kramers chose a great start for their new marriage—blessing God by serving others. The apostle Paul encouraged the Christians of Galatia: "Through love serve one another" (Galatians 5:13 NKJV). Some of them believed that the ceremonial practices of the Old Testament were still binding on the church. So Paul reminded them that salvation is by grace through faith. It is by faith we live out our new life in Christ. He reminded them that the law was fulfilled in this: "Love your neighbor as yourself" (v. 14).

As followers of Jesus, we're here to serve Him out of love—to "bless God for blessing us."

—*Anne Cetas*

———

I love you, LORD, my strength. Psalm 18:1

MY PRINCE

Read: Ephesians 5:22-33

Husbands, love your wives, just as Christ loved the church and gave himself up for her. —EPHESIANS 5:25

People around the world reacted with shock in September 2006 when news broke that Steve Irwin, the "Crocodile Hunter," had died. His enthusiasm for life and for God's creatures was contagious, making him a favorite personality worldwide.

When his wife Terri was interviewed shortly after Steve's death, her love for him was obvious as she said through her tears, "I've lost my prince." What an affectionate way to memorialize her husband! She saw him as her prince and her best friend.

Too often today the husband-wife relationship is viewed as anything but the tender one Terri and Steve must have shared. We often see bitterness, insults, and animosity presented in the media as the norm. How much more desirable it is to see true love—to see a husband unashamedly cherish his wife, to unselfishly be her "prince."

How can a husband continue to love his wife in a more princely way? Try these suggestions: Listen—enjoy those tender times when she can unburden her heart without fear. Love life—find ways to add fun to your marriage. Lead spiritually—guide the way into prayer and intimate fellowship with the Lord.

—*Dave Branon*

Husbands, love your wives. Ephesians 5:25

STORM CLOUDS

Read: Romans 8:18-30

For our light and momentary troubles are achieving for us an eternal glory that far outweighs them all. —2 CORINTHIANS 4:17

I was feeling down about some circumstances the other day and wondering how I might lift my spirits. I pulled from my shelf the book *Life Is Like Licking Honey Off a Thorn* by Susan Lenzkes, and I read this: "We take the laughter and the tears however they come, and let our God of reality make sense of it all."

Lenzkes says some people are optimists who "camp in pleasures and good memories," denying the brokenness. Others are pessimists who "focus on life's losses, losing joy and victory in the process." But people of faith are realists who "receive it all all the good and bad of life—and repeatedly choose to know that God really loves us and is constantly at work for our good and His glory."

As I read, I looked outside and noticed dark clouds and a steady rain. A little later, a friendly wind came up and blew the clouds away. Suddenly the skies were bright blue. The storms of life blow in and out like that.

By faith we cling to God's promise of Romans 8:28. And we recall that "our light and momentary troubles are achieving for us an eternal glory that far outweighs them all" (2 Corinthians 4:17). God loves us, and He's getting us ready for the day when skies will be forever blue.

—*Anne Cetas*

Whoever claims to love God yet hates a brother or sister is a liar. 1 John 4:20

LEARNING TO LOVE

Read: 1 Corinthians 13

Follow the way of love and eagerly desire gifts of the Spirit,
especially prophecy. —1 CORINTHIANS 14:1

Love does more than make "the world go 'round," as an old song says. It also makes us immensely vulnerable. From time to time, we may say to ourselves: "Why love when others do not show appreciation?" or "Why love and open myself up to hurt?" But the apostle Paul gives a clear and simple reason to pursue love: "These three remain: faith, hope and love. But the greatest of these is love. Follow the way of love" (1 Corinthians 13:13–14:1).

"Love is an activity, the essential activity of God himself," writes Bible commentator C. K. Barrett, "and when men love either Him or their fellow-men, they are doing (however imperfectly) what God does." And God is pleased when we act like Him.

To begin following the way of love, think about how you might live out the characteristics listed in 1 Corinthians 13:4–7. For example, how can I show my child the same patience God shows me? How can I show kindness and respect for my parents? What does it mean to look out for the interests of others when I am at work? When something good happens to my friend, do I rejoice with her or am I envious?

As we "follow the way of love," we'll find ourselves often turning to God, the source of love, and to Jesus, the greatest example of love. Only then will we gain a deeper knowledge of what true love is and find the strength to love others as God loves us.

—*Poh Fang Chia*

Love is kind.

1 Corinthians 13:4

)(

LOVE AND LIGHT

Read Deuteronomy 11:8-15

The land you are crossing the Jordan to take possession of is a land of mountains and valleys that drinks rain from heaven. It is a land the LORD your God cares for; the eyes of the LORD your God are continually on it from the beginning of the year to its end.
—DEUTERONOMY 11:11–12

I love it when I see friends begin to plan their summer vegetable gardens. Some get an early start by planting seeds indoors where they can control the conditions and provide the best environment for sprouting. After the danger of frost has passed, they will transplant the seedlings outdoors. Once the garden is planted, the work of weeding, feeding, watering, and guarding against rodents and insects begins. Producing food is a lot of work.

Moses reminded the Israelites of this before they entered the Promised Land. While living in Egypt, they had to do the hard work of irrigating crops by hand (Deuteronomy 11:10), but in the place where God was taking them He promised to ease their work by sending spring and autumn rains: "I will send rain on your land in its season, both autumn and spring rains" (v. 14). The only condition was that they "faithfully obey the commands" He gave them—"to love the LORD your God and to serve him with all your heart and with all your soul" (v. 13). The Lord was taking His people to a place where their obedience and His blessing would make them a light to those around them.

God wants the same for us and from us: He wants our love to be displayed in our obedience so we can be His light to people around us. The love and obedience we have to offer, though, is far less than He deserves. But He is our provider, blessing us and enabling us to be a light that the world will notice.

—*Julie Ackerman Link*

Love is not self-seeking. 1 Corinthians 13:5

CAN YOU HELP?

Read James 2:14-20

In the same way, faith by itself, if it is not accompanied by action, is dead.
—JAMES 2:17

The administrators of the high school in Barrow, Alaska, were tired of seeing students get into trouble and drop out at a rate of fifty percent. To keep students interested, they started a football team, which offered them a chance to develop personal skills, practice teamwork, and learn life lessons. The problem with football in Barrow, which is farther north than Iceland, is that it's hard to plant a grass field. So they competed on a gravel and dirt field.

Four thousand miles away in Florida, a woman named Cathy Parker heard about the football team and their dangerous field. Feeling that God was prompting her to help and impressed by the positive changes she saw in the students, she went to work. About a year later, the school dedicated its new field, complete with a beautiful artificial-turf playing surface. She had raised thousands of dollars to help some kids she didn't even know.

This is not about football—or money. It is about remembering "to do good and to share" (Hebrews 13:16). The apostle James reminds us that we demonstrate our faith by our actions (2:18). The needs in our world are varied and overwhelming. But when we love our neighbor as ourselves, as Jesus said (Mark 12:31), we reach people with God's love.

—*Dave Branon*

Do everything in love. 1 Corinthians 16:14

GOD'S LOVE THROUGH ME

Read: 1 Corinthians 13

*Love never fails. But where there are prophecies, they will cease;
where there are tongues, they will be stilled; where there is knowledge,
it will pass away.* —1 CORINTHIANS 13:8

During a devotional session at a conference, our leader asked us to read aloud 1 Corinthians 13:4–8, and substitute the word "Jesus" for "love." It seemed so natural to say, "Jesus is patient, Jesus is kind; Jesus does not envy; Jesus does not boast, is not proud; does not dishonor others, is not self-seeking . . . . Jesus never fails."

Then our leader said, "Read the passage aloud and say your name instead of Jesus." We laughed nervously at the suggestion. "I want you to begin now," the leader said. Quietly, haltingly I said the words that felt so untrue: "David is not self-seeking, is not easily angered, does not delight in evil but rejoices with the truth. David never fails."

The exercise caused me to ask, "How am I hindering God from expressing His love through me?" Do I think that other expressions of faith are more important? Paul declared that from God's perspective, eloquent speech, deep spiritual understanding, lavish generosity, and self-sacrifice are worthless when not accompanied by love (vv. 1–3).

God longs to express His great heart of love for others through us. Will we allow Him to do it?

—*David McCasland*

Greater love has no one than this: to lay down one's life for one's friends. John 15:13

LOVE YOUR NEIGHBOR

Read: Romans 13:8-11

For the entire law is fulfilled in keeping this one command: "Love your neighbor as yourself." —GALATIANS 5:14

An anthropologist was winding up several months of research in a small village, the story is told. While waiting for a ride to the airport for his return flight home, he decided to pass the time by making up a game for some children. His idea was to create a race for a basket of fruit and candy that he placed near a tree. But when he gave the signal to run, no one made a dash for the finish line. Instead the children joined hands and ran together to the tree.

When asked why they chose to run as a group rather than each racing for the prize, a little girl spoke up and said: "How could one of us be happy when all of the others are sad?" Because these children cared about each other, they wanted all to share the basket of fruit and candy.

After years of studying the law of Moses, the apostle Paul found that all of God's laws could be summed up in one: "Love your neighbor as yourself" (Galatians 5:14; see also Romans 13:9). In Christ, Paul saw not only the reason to encourage, comfort, and care for one another but also the spiritual enablement to do it.

Because He cares for us, we care for each other.

—*Mart DeHaan*

Perfect love drives out fear. 1 John 4:18

PINK SHEEP

Read: John 10:7-18

By this everyone will know that you are my disciples,
if you love one another. —JOHN 13:35

While traveling on a road from Glasgow to Edinburgh, Scotland, I was enjoying the beautiful, pastoral countryside when a rather humorous sight captured my attention. There, on a small hilltop, was a rather large flock of pink sheep.

I know that sheep owners mark their animals with dots of spray paint to identify them—but these sheep really stood out. The owner had fully covered every animal with pink coloring. Everyone knew who those sheep belonged to.

Scripture calls followers of Christ "sheep," and they too have a unique identifying mark. What is the "pink coloring" in a Christ-follower's life? How can someone be identified as Jesus's own?

In the gospel of John, Jesus, the Good Shepherd, told us what that identifier is: Love. "Love one another. As I have loved you . . . . By this everyone will know that you are my disciples, if you love one another" (John 13:34–35).

In words and deeds, a believer should show love to all those around. "Dear friends," John writes, "since God so loved us, we also ought to love one another" (1 John 4:11). A Christian's love for others should be as obvious as pink wool on a flock of Scottish sheep.

—*Dave Branon*

This is love: not that we loved God,
but that he loved us and sent his Son
as an atoning sacrifice.

1 John 4:10

GOD'S EMBRACE

Read: Romans 12:3-11

Be devoted to one another in love. Honor one another above yourselves.
—ROMANS 12:10

Soon after her family left for the evening, Carol started to think that her hospital room must be the loneliest place in the world. Nighttime had fallen, her fears about her illness were back, and she felt overwhelming despair as she lay there alone.

Closing her eyes, she began to talk to God: "O Lord, I know I am not really alone. You are here with me. Please calm my heart and give me peace. Let me feel your arms around me, holding me."

As she prayed, Carol felt her fears beginning to subside. And when she opened her eyes, she looked up to see the warm, sparkling eyes of her friend Marge, who reached out to encircle her in a big hug. Carol felt as if God himself were holding her tightly.

God often uses fellow believers to show us His love. "In Christ we, though many, form one body. . . . We have different gifts, according to the grace given to each of us" (Romans 12:5–6). We serve others "with the strength God provides, so that in all things God may be praised through Jesus Christ" (1 Peter 4:11).

When we show love and compassion in simple, practical ways, we are a part of God's ministry to His people.

—*Cindy Hess Kasper*

Walk in the way of love. Ephesians 5:2

A GOOD NEIGHBOR POLICY

Read: Leviticus 19:13-18

" 'Do not seek revenge or bear a grudge against anyone among your people,
but love your neighbor as yourself. I am the LORD.' "
—LEVITICUS 19:18

One morning my wife and I awoke to find a note from our neighbors on our front door. It read in part, "We've gone away until tomorrow night. Please look after Cleo [the family dog] for us. If she howls and wants to go inside, a spare key is hanging on a nail by the garage door. Thanks." I was glad to read that note because it meant that a strong bridge of trust had been built between us in the two years since they had moved in.

In our Scripture reading, the Israelites were instructed not to rob their neighbors (Leviticus 19:13), to judge fairly (v. 15), not to do anything that would threaten the life of their neighbors (v. 16), and to love and forgive them (v. 18). In this way they would give witness to the nations that Jehovah was the true God and that those who worshiped Him were loving, honest, and just in their personal relationships and in their business dealings.

What was true for Israel is also true for Christians. We too should love our neighbors, and that includes more than just the people who live next door. Jesus defined our neighbor as anyone in need (Luke 10:29–37).

So let's look for ways to develop genuine friendships by lending a hand in time of need. It might mean an emergency run to the hospital, or giving a neighbor a half-gallon of milk when we're running low ourselves.

A good neighbor policy may even help bring someone to Christ.

—*David Egner*

If I do not have love, I gain nothing. 1 Corinthians 13:3

WHAT IS LOVE?

Read: Psalm 103:1-14

This is love: not that we loved God, but that he loved us and sent his Son as an atoning sacrifice for our sins. —1 JOHN 4:10

When asked, "What is love?" children have some great answers. Noelle, age seven, said, "Love is when you tell a guy you like his shirt, then he wears it every day." Rebecca, who is eight, answered, "Since my grandmother got arthritis, she can't bend over and polish her toenails anymore. So my grandfather does it for her all the time, even after his hands got arthritis too. That's love." Jessica, also eight, concluded, "You really shouldn't say 'I love you' unless you mean it. But if you mean it, you should say it a lot. People forget."

Sometimes we need to be reminded that God loves us. We focus on the difficulties of life and wonder, *Where's the love?* But if we pause and consider all that God has done for us, we remember how much we are loved by God, who is love (1 John 4:8–10).

Psalm 103 lists the "benefits" God showers on us in love: He forgives our sin (v. 3), satisfies us with good things (v. 5), and executes righteousness and justice (v. 6). He is slow to anger and abounds in mercy (v. 8). He doesn't deal with us as our sins deserve (v. 10), and He has removed our sin as far as the east is from the west (v. 12). He has not forgotten us!

What is love? God is love, and He's pouring out that love on you and me.

—*Anne Cetas*

There is no fear in love. 1 John 4:18

HIS LOVING PRESENCE

Read: Hebrews 13:1-6

*Keep your lives free from the love of money and be content
with what you have, because God has said, "Never will I leave you;
never will I forsake you."* —HEBREWS 13:5

Our hearts sank when we learned that our good friend Cindy had been diagnosed with cancer. Cindy was a vibrant person whose life blessed all who crossed her path. My wife and I rejoiced when she went into remission, but a few months later her cancer returned with a vengeance. In our minds she was too young to die. Her husband told me about her last hours. When she was weak and hardly able to talk, Cindy whispered to him, "Just be with me." What she wanted more than anything in those dark moments was his loving presence.

The writer to the Hebrews comforted his readers by quoting Deuteronomy 31:6, where the people were told that God "will never leave [them] nor forsake [them]" (see Hebrews 13:5). In the darkest moments of life, the assurance of God's loving presence gives us confidence that we are not alone. He gives us the grace to endure, the wisdom to know He is working, and the assurance that Christ can "empathize with our weaknesses" (4:15).

Together let's embrace the blessing of His loving presence so we can confidently say, "The Lord is my helper; I will not be afraid" (13:6).

—*Joe Stowell*

**By this everyone will know that you are my disciples, if you love
one another. John 13:35**

THE GALLERY OF GOD

Read: Psalm 100

The LORD is good and his love endures forever;
his faithfulness continues through all generations. —PSALM 100:5

Psalm 100 is like a work of art that helps us celebrate our unseen God. While the focus of our worship is beyond view, His people make Him known.

Imagine the artist with brush and palette working the colorful words of this psalm onto a canvas. What emerges before our eyes is a world—"all the earth"—shouting for joy to the Lord (v. 1). *Joy.* Because it is the delight of our God to redeem us from death. "For the *joy* that was set before Him," Jesus endured the cross (Hebrews 12:2 NKJV).

As our eyes move across the canvas, we see an all-world choir of countless members singing "with gladness" and "joyful songs" (Psalm 100:2). Our heavenly Father's heart is pleased when His people worship Him for who He is and what He has done.

Then we see images of ourselves, fashioned from dust in the hands of our Creator and led like sheep into green pasture (v. 3). We, His people, have a loving Shepherd.

Finally, we see God's great and glorious dwelling place—and the gates through which His rescued people enter His unseen presence, while giving Him thanks and praise (v. 4).

What a picture, inspired by our God! Our good, loving, and faithful God. No wonder it will take forever to enjoy His greatness!

—*Dave Branon*

Whoever does not love does not know God, because God is love.

1 John 4:8

⋊⋉

MAX AND THE ORPHANED CALF

Read: 1 Thessalonians 2:1-7

We were like young children among you. Just as a nursing mother cares for her children, so we cared for you. —1 THESSALONIANS 2:7–8

My friend Max runs a small farm as a hobby. Recently when he checked on the cows he is raising, he was surprised to see a newborn calf! When he bought the cows, he had no idea one was pregnant. Sadly, the mother cow had complications and died shortly after her calf was born. Immediately, Max purchased some powdered milk so he could feed the calf from a bottle. "The calf thinks I'm its mother!" Max told me.

The tender story of Max's new role with the calf reminded me of how Paul likened himself to a caring mother in dealing with the believers at Thessalonica: "We were gentle among you," he said, "just as a nursing mother cherishes her own children" (1 Thessalonians 2:7 NKJV).

Paul adopted a nurturing attitude when teaching people. He knew believers needed the "milk of the word" for spiritual growth (1 Peter 2:2 NKJV). But he also gave special attention to the concerns of those he cared for. "We dealt with each of you as a father deals with his own children," Paul said, "encouraging, comforting and urging you to live lives worthy of God" (1 Thessalonians 2:11–12).

As we serve each other, may we serve with the tender loving care of our Savior, encouraging each other in our spiritual journey (Hebrews 10:24).

—Dennis Fisher

Keep on loving one another as brothers and sisters. Hebrews 13:1

JESUS AND THE GOLDEN RULE

Read: Matthew 7:7-12

*Therefore, whatever you want men to do to you, do also to them,
for this is the Law and the Prophets.* —MATTHEW 7:12 NKJV

The concept of The Golden Rule—treat others as you would like to be treated—appears in many religions. So what makes Jesus's version of the saying so exceptional?

Its uniqueness lies in a single word, "therefore," which signals the generosity of our heavenly Father. Here is what Jesus said: "If you then, being evil, know how to give good gifts to your children, how much more will your Father who is in heaven give good things to those who ask Him! *Therefore*, whatever you want men to do to you, do also to them" (Matthew 7:11–12, NKJV, italics added).

All of us fall short of what we know to be true: We do not love others the way God loves us. Jesus lived out that admirable ethic with perfect love by living and dying for all our sins.

We have a loving, giving Father who set aside His own self-interest to reveal the full measure of His love through His Son Jesus. God's generosity is the dynamic by which we treat others as we would like to be treated. We love and give to others because He first loved us (1 John 4:19).

Our heavenly Father asks us to live up to His commands, but He also gives us His power and love to carry it out. We need only to ask Him for it.

—David Roper

Serve one another humbly in love. Galatians 5:13

LOVE IS FOR LOSERS

Read: 1 Corinthians 13

And now these three remain: faith, hope and love. But the greatest of these is love. —1 CORINTHIANS 13:13

You can learn a lot about a person by what his or her T-shirt says. Recently, one of these messages caught my attention as I walked through a local shopping mall. A young woman wore a bright red T-shirt that said, "Love Is for Losers." Maybe she thought it was clever or provocative, even funny. Or perhaps she had been hurt by a relationship and had pulled away from others rather than risk being hurt again. Either way, the T-shirt got me thinking.

Is love for losers? The fact is, when we love, we take risks. People could very well hurt us, disappoint us, or even leave us. Love can lead to loss.

The Bible, though, challenges us to higher ground in loving others. In 1 Corinthians 13, Paul describes what it means to live out God's kind of love. The person who exercises godly love doesn't do so for personal benefit or gain but rather "always protects, always trusts, always hopes, always perseveres" (13:7). Why? Because godly love endures beyond life's hurts by pulling us relentlessly toward the never-diminishing care of the Father.

So, perhaps love is for losers—for it is in times of loss and disappointment that we need God's love the most. Even in our struggles, we know that "love never fails" (1 Corinthians 13:8).

—*Bill Crowder*

Because of the LORD's great love we are not consumed, for his compassions never fail. Lamentations 3:22

AN ATHEIST'S WITNESS

Read: 1 John 3:11-18

Jesus replied: "'Love the Lord your God with all your heart and with all your soul and with all your mind.' "—MATTHEW 22:37

Aware that love of God and neighbor is a central teaching of Scripture, I did my doctoral dissertation on "The Concept of Love in the Psychology of Sigmund Freud." I learned that this influential thinker, who had no faith in God, nevertheless stressed the supreme importance of love.

Freud wrote, for example, that the best way to "escape from the cares of life" and "forget real misery" is to follow the path "that expects all satisfaction to come from loving and being loved." In this point, Freud was in agreement with the Bible, which focuses on love.

Scripture teaches that "God is love" (1 John 4:8). It also teaches the importance of "faith expressing itself through love" (Galatians 5:6). So the great problem we all face is how to rid ourselves of sinful self-love while sincerely loving God and our neighbor (Matthew 22:37–39; 1 John 3:14). The gospel—with its message of the life-transforming love of Christ—provides the only answer to that problem. Paul declared in Romans 5:5, "God's love has been poured out into our hearts through the Holy Spirit."

Have you experienced the infilling of God's love? Only when you trust Jesus as Savior will the Holy Spirit of love begin to flow in and through you.

—Vernon Grounds

**For God so loved the world that he gave his one and only son.
John 3:16**

LETTING GOD CHOOSE

Read: Genesis 13:9-13

So Lot chose for himself the whole plain of the Jordan and set out toward the east. The two men parted company. —GENESIS 13:11

We may have secret longings too deep to utter to others—perhaps a desire for marriage, or a work or ministry we'd like to perform, or a special place to serve. We can take those longings to God: "Lord, You must choose for me. I will not choose for myself."

Genesis 13:10–11 tells us that Lot made his own choice about a desire he had. He "looked around and saw that the whole plain of the Jordan toward Zoar was well watered, like the garden of the LORD . . . . So Lot chose for himself the whole plain of the Jordan."

The plain of the Jordan, with its rich soil and copious water supply, looked best to Lot. But the land was polluted with wickedness (v. 13). Pastor Ray Stedman wrote that "Lot, presuming to run his own life, 'chose for himself,' and, deceived by what he saw, stumbled blindly into heartache and judgment. Abram, on the other hand, was content to let God choose for him. . . . Abram saw it in its true light." Lot chose for himself and lost everything—his family, his fortune, his favor with man.

It is always the best course for us to let God choose and to follow His direction, knowing as we do that all our heavenly Father's choices are prompted by infinite wisdom and love.

—*David Roper*

For the LORD loves the just.

Psalm 37:28

XK

UNCHANGING LOVE

Read: James 1:12-20

*Every good and perfect gift is from above, coming down from the Father
of the heavenly lights, who does not change like shifting shadows.*
—JAMES 1:17

At a wedding I attended, the bride's grandfather quoted from memory a moving selection of Scripture about the relationship of husband and wife. Then a friend of the couple read "Sonnet 116" by William Shakespeare. The minister conducting the ceremony used a phrase from that sonnet to illustrate the kind of love that should characterize a Christian marriage: "Love is not love which alters when it alteration finds." The poet is saying that true love does not change with circumstances.

The minister noted the many changes this couple would experience during their life together, including health and the inevitable effects of age. Then he challenged them to cultivate the true biblical love that neither falters nor fails in spite of the alterations that would surely come their way.

As I witnessed the joy and excitement of this young couple, a verse came to mind from James: "Every good and perfect gift is from above, coming down from the Father of the heavenly lights, who does not change like shifting shadows" (1:17). God never changes, and neither does His love for us. We are recipients of a perfect love from our heavenly Father, who has loved us "with an everlasting love" (Jeremiah 31:3).

We are called to accept God's unfailing love, to allow it to shape our lives, and to extend it to others.

—*David McCasland*

Love each other as I have loved you. John 15:12

YOU ARE NEVER ALONE

Read: John 14:15-21

I will not leave you as orphans; I will come to you. —JOHN 14:18

Jesus is just as real today as He was when He walked on this earth. Even though He doesn't move among us physically, by the Holy Spirit He is here, there, everywhere—a continuous, living presence—outside of us and inside of us.

That may be a terrifying thought for some. Perhaps you don't like yourself, or you're contemplating all the bad things you've done. Insecurity and sin can create a sense of fear, awkwardness, and clumsiness in Jesus's presence. But think of what you know about Him.

Despite what you are or what you may have done, He loves you (Romans 5:8; 1 John 4:7–11). He will never leave you nor forsake you (John 14:18; Hebrews 13:5). Others may not think much of you or invite you to spend time with them, but Jesus does (Matthew 11:28). Others may not like the way you look, but He looks at your heart (1 Samuel 16:7). Others may think you're a bother because you're old and in the way, but He will love you to the end (Romans 8:35–39).

Jesus loves you in spite of all the conditions that cause others to turn away. He wants to change you to be like Him, but He loves you as you are and will never abandon you. You are family; you will never, ever be alone.

—David Roper

———

Whoever pursues righteousness and love finds life, prosperity and honor. Proverbs 21:21

GOD LOVES ATHEISTS

Read: Isaiah 55:1-7

Let the wicked forsake their ways and the unrighteous their thoughts.
Let them turn to the LORD, and he will have mercy on them, and to our
God, for he will freely pardon. —ISAIAH 55:7

Madalyn Murray O'Hair was perhaps the most notorious atheist of the 1900s. Often profane and sarcastic, she was a powerful debater who shouted down her religious opponents.

After O'Hair mysteriously disappeared in 1995, her diaries were auctioned to pay back taxes she owed the federal government. They reveal an unhappy human being who didn't trust even the members of the American Atheists Association. She passed this harsh judgment on herself: "I have failed in marriage, motherhood, and as a politician." Yet she yearned for acceptance and friendship. In her diary she wrote six times, "Somebody, somewhere, love me."

Instead of viewing atheists like O'Hair as enemies, we should see them as people God loves. They have a void in their lives that only He can fill. In Isaiah 55:7 we hear God calling out to the godless, inviting them to come to Him and experience His mercy and forgiveness.

We who have experienced the Lord's grace have an opportunity to proclaim His invitation to others. Even in the face of hostility, we can tell those who have turned their backs on God that if they respond to His love for them they will find peace for their troubled hearts.

—*Vernon Grounds*

Let your face shine on your servant; save me in your unfailing love. Psalm 31:16

LOVE IN THE SKY

Read: Romans 6:1-11

Now if we died with Christ, we believe that we will also live with him.
—ROMANS 6:8

My husband and I were at a public swimming pool when the people around us started staring into the sky. A small plane was emitting smoke in the form of letters. As we watched, the pilot spelled out the letters: "I L-O-V-E." People began speculating: Maybe it was to be a marriage proposal. Perhaps a romantic man is standing nearby on a balcony with his girl-friend and will soon pop the Will-you-marry-me? question. We kept gazing upward: "I L-O-V-E Y-O-U J-E-." I heard young girls guessing: "I bet it will be Jen or maybe Jessica." He kept spelling. No. It was: "J-E-S-U-S." The pilot was declaring love for Jesus for many people to see.

A friend of mine often ends his prayers with "I love you, Lord." He says, "I can't help but say 'I love you' after all He's done for me." In Romans 6:1–11, our Bible text for today, the apostle Paul tells us some of what Jesus has done for us that deserves our love: He was crucified, buried, and raised to life. Because of that, those of us who have put our faith in Jesus now have a new life (v. 4), we no longer have to be controlled by sin or fear of death (vv. 6, 9), and one day we too will be resurrected to live with Him forever (v. 8).

No wonder we say, "I love you, Jesus!"

—*Anne Cetas*

Whoever lives in love, lives in God. 1 John 4:16

REMINDERS OF LOVE

Read: John 19:1–7; 16–18

Whoever does not love does not know God, because God is love.
—1 JOHN 4:8

After the US entered World War II in 1941, Estelle tried to talk her boyfriend Sidney out of joining the Army. But he enlisted and began his training in April of the following year. For the next three years he wrote her love letters—525 in all. Then in March 1945, she learned that her beloved fiancé had been killed in combat.

Although Estelle did eventually marry, the memories of her first love lived in her heart. To honor that love, she published a book of Sidney's wartime correspondence more than sixty years later.

Like those letters, the Lord has left us with reminders of His love—the Scriptures. He says: "I have loved you with an everlasting love; I have drawn you with unfailing kindness" (Jeremiah 31:3).

"As the Father has loved me, so have I loved you. Now remain in my love" (John 15:9).

The Bible also tells us that "Christ loved the church and gave himself up for her" (Ephesians 5:25).

"[Jesus] gave himself for us to redeem us" (Titus 2:14).

"God is love" (1 John 4:8).

Read God's Word—His love letters to you—often and be reminded that Jesus loves you and died for you.

—*Anne Cetas*

Mercy, peace and love
be yours in abundance.

Jude 1:2

XX

CHANGING ENEMIES INTO FRIENDS

Read: Matthew 5:43-48

But I tell you, love your enemies and pray for those who persecute you.
—MATTHEW 5:44

During the US Civil War, hatred became entrenched between the North and South. In one instance, President Abraham Lincoln was criticized for speaking of benevolent treatment for the Southern rebels. The critic reminded Lincoln that there was a war going on, the Confederates were the enemy, and they should be destroyed. But Lincoln wisely responded, "I destroy my enemies when I make them my friends."

Lincoln's comment is insightful. In many ways it reflects Jesus's teaching in the Sermon on the Mount: "I tell you, love your enemies and pray for those who persecute you, that you may be children of your Father in heaven. He causes his sun to rise on the evil and the good, and sends on the righteous and the unrighteous" (Matthew 5:44–45).

We will encounter difficult people in our lives—some on whom we will need to set limits. But to give in to the temptation to undermine or hurt them in any way is not God's way. Instead, we should pray for them, show consideration, look out for their best interests, and emphasize the positive. This may result in changing an enemy into a friend.

Not everyone will respond positively to us, but we can pray and plan for a more harmonious relationship. What difficult person can you start befriending?

—*Dennis Fisher*

Love your enemies and pray for those who persecute you.
Matthew 5:44

HELPING LOVE GROW

Read: 1 Corinthians 13

[Love] does not dishonor others, it is not self-seeking, it is not easily angered, it keeps no record of wrongs. —1 CORINTHIANS 13:5

A young man told his father, "Dad, I'm going to get married."

"How do you know you're ready to get married, Ron?" asked the father. "Are you in love?"

"I sure am," he replied.

The father then asked, "Ron, how do you know you're in love?"

"Last night as I was kissing my girlfriend goodnight, her dog bit me and I didn't feel the pain until I got home!"

Ron has got that loving feeling, but he has a lot of growing to do. Vernon Grounds, a former writer for *Our Daily Bread*, who was married for more than 70 years before his death in 2010, shared these points about how to grow in love:

Ponder God's love in Christ. Take time to reflect on how He gave His life for you. Read about Him in the Gospels, and thank Him.

Pray for the love of God. Ask Him to give you an understanding of His love and to teach you how to live that out in your relationships with your spouse and others (1 Corinthians 13).

Practice the love of God. Give of yourself. A newlywed told me he thinks love is practical. He said, "My responsibility is to make life easier for my spouse." The other, tougher side of love is to challenge each other to act in godly ways.

Love will grow when we ponder love, pray for love, and practice love.

—*Anne Cetas*

Christ's love compels us. 2 Corinthians 5:14

LISTENING WITH LOVE

Read: Luke 18:9-14

"I tell you that this man, rather than the other, went home justified before God. For all those who exalt themselves will be humbled, and those who humble themselves will be exalted." —LUKE 18:14

One August evening in Vermont, a young missionary spoke at our small church. The country where he and his wife served was in religious turmoil, and it was considered too dangerous for children. In one of his stories, he told us about a heart-wrenching episode when his daughter pleaded with him not to leave her behind at a boarding school.

I was a new dad at that time, having recently been blessed with a daughter, and the story upset me. *How could loving parents leave their daughter alone like that?* I thought to myself. By the time the talk was finished, I was so worked up that I ignored the offer to visit with the missionary. I charged out of the church, saying out loud as I left: "I'm sure glad I'm not like . . ."

In that instant, the Holy Spirit stopped me cold. I couldn't even finish the sentence. Here I was, saying almost word for word what the Pharisee said to God: "I thank you that I am not like other people" (Luke 18:11). How disappointed I was in myself! How disappointed God must have been! Since that evening, I've asked God to help me listen to others with humility and restraint as they pour their hearts out in confession, profession, or pain.

—*Randy Kilgore*

———

Love covers over all wrongs. Proverbs 10:12

AN AMAZING LOVE

Read: Malachi 1:1-10; 4:5-6

"I have loved you," says the LORD. "But you ask, 'How have you loved us?' "Was not Esau Jacob's brother?" declares the LORD. "Yet I have loved Jacob." —MALACHI 1:2

The final major historic acts of the Old Testament are described in Ezra and Nehemiah as God allowed the people of Israel to return from exile and resettle in Jerusalem. The City of David was repopulated with Hebrew families, a new temple was built, and the wall was repaired.

And that brings us to Malachi. This prophet, who was most likely a contemporary of Nehemiah, brings the written portion of the Old Testament to a close. Notice the first thing he said to the people of Israel: " 'I have loved you,' says the LORD." And look at their response: "How have you loved us?" (1:2).

Amazing, isn't it? Their history had proven God's faithfulness, yet after hundreds of years in which God continually provided for His chosen people in both miraculous and mundane ways, they wondered how He had shown His love. As the book continues, Malachi reminds the people of their unfaithfulness (see vv. 6–8). They had a long historical pattern of God's provision for them, followed by their disobedience, followed by God's discipline.

It was time, soon, for a new way. The prophet hints at it in Malachi 4:5–6. The Messiah would be coming. There was hope ahead for a Savior who would show His love and pay the penalty for sin once and for all.

That Messiah indeed has come! Malachi's hope is now a reality in Jesus.

—Dave Branon

These three remain: faith, hope and love. But the greatest of these is love. 1 Corinthians 13:33

HOW GOD SHOWS HIS LOVE

Read: John 13:1-17

I have set you an example that you should do as I have done for you.
—JOHN 13:15

Martha, a twenty-six-year-old woman with ALS (amyotrophic lateral sclerosis), needed help. When a group of ladies from Evanston, Illinois, heard about her, they jumped into action. They began to give round-the-clock nursing care. They bathed her, fed her, prayed for her, and witnessed to her. Martha, who had not received Christ as her Savior and couldn't understand how a loving God could let her get ALS, saw His love in these women and eventually became a Christian. She is with the Lord today because sixteen women, following Jesus's example, personified God's love.

The love of God was visibly demonstrated in Jesus when He was here on Earth. In stooping to wash the feet of His disciples, He mirrored the submissive step He took when He left heaven and became a man. He healed the sick and endured bitter hatred as His reward. He died like a criminal on a Roman cross. His endurance and these acts of kindness reflect God's love, for Jesus said, "Anyone who has seen me has seen the Father" (John 14:9).

Jesus is no longer with us in His physical body—He now sits at God's right hand in heaven. So, if God's love is to be embodied today, it must be done through Christians. Is it being done through you?

—*Herb Vander Lugt*

To your name be the glory,

because of your love and faithfulness.

Psalm 115:1

𝕏

GOD SO LOVED . . .

Read: John 3:13-19

Jesus said, "Father, forgive them, for they do not know what they are doing." And they divided up his clothes by casting lots. —LUKE 23:34

July 28, 2014, marked the 100th anniversary of the beginning of World War I. In the British media many discussions and documentaries recalled the start of that four-year conflict. Even the TV program *Mr. Selfridge,* which is based on an actual department store in London, included an episode set in 1914 that showed young male employees lining up to volunteer for the army. As I observed these portrayals of self-sacrifice, I felt a lump in my throat. The soldiers they depicted had been so young, so eager, and so unlikely to return from the horror of the trenches.

Although Jesus didn't go off to war to defeat an earthly foe, He did go to the cross to defeat the ultimate enemy—sin and death. Jesus came to earth to demonstrate God's love in action and to die a horrendous death so that we could be forgiven of our sins. And He was even prepared to forgive the men who flogged and crucified Him (Luke 23:34). He conquered death by His resurrection and now we can become part of God's forever family (John 3:13–16).

Anniversaries and memorials remind us of important historical events and heroic deeds. The cross reminds us of the pain of Jesus's death and the beauty of His sacrifice for our salvation.

—*Marion Stroud*

May the Lord make your love increase and overflow for each other. 1 Thessalonians 3:12

A MATTER OF LOVE

Read: Mark 12:28-34

Love the LORD your God with all your heart and with all your soul and with all your strength. —DEUTERONOMY 6:5

"Where intellect and emotion clash, the heart often has the greater wisdom," wrote the authors of *A General Theory of Love*. In the past, they say, people believed that the mind should rule the heart, but science has now discovered the opposite to be true. "Who we are and who we become depends, in part, on whom we love."

Those familiar with Scripture recognize this as an ancient truth, not a new discovery. The most important commandment God gave to His people gives the heart the prominent place. "Love the LORD your God with all your heart and with all your soul and with all your strength" (Deuteronomy 6:5). Not until the gospels of Mark and Luke do we learn that Jesus added the word *mind* (Mark 12:30; Luke 10:27). So, what scientists are just now discovering, the Bible taught all along.

Those of us who follow Christ also know the importance of whom we love. When we obey the greatest commandment and make God the object of our love, we can be assured of having a purpose that transcends anything we could imagine or our strength could achieve. When our desire for God dominates our hearts, our minds will stay focused on ways to serve Him, and our actions will further His kingdom on earth and in heaven.

—*Julie Ackerman Link*

————

Love your neighbor as yourself. Mark 12:31

DEEPLY LOVED

Read: Matthew 6:25-34

Look at the birds of the air; they do not sow or reap or store away in barns, and yet your heavenly Father feeds them. Are you not much more valuable than they? —MATTHEW 6:26

Years ago I had an office in Boston that looked out on the Granary Burying Ground where many prominent American heroes are buried. There one can find the gravestones for John Hancock and Samuel Adams, two signers of the Declaration of Independence, and just a few feet beyond that is Paul Revere's marker.

But no one really knows *where* in this burial ground each body is buried because the stones have been moved many times—sometimes to make the grounds more picturesque and other times so lawn mowers could fit between them. And while the Granary features approximately 2,300 markers, closer to 5,000 people are buried there! Even in death, it seems, some people are not fully known.

There may be times when we feel as if we are like those unmarked residents of the Granary, unknown and unseen. Loneliness can make us feel unseen by others—and maybe even by God. But we must remind ourselves that even though we may feel forgotten by our Creator God, we are not. God not only made us in His image (Genesis 1:26–27), but He also values each of us individually and sent His Son to save us (John 3:16).

Even in our darkest hours, we can rest in the knowledge we are never alone, for our loving God is with us.

—*Randy Kilgore*

———

As I have loved you, you must love one another. John 13:34

THE TREE OF LOVE

Read: Matthew 27:27-35

"He himself bore our sins" in his body on the cross, so that we might die to sins and live for righteousness; "by his wounds you have been healed."
—1 PETER 2:24

The corkscrew willow tree stood vigil over our backyard for more than twenty years. It shaded all four of our children as they played in the yard, and it provided shelter for the neighborhood squirrels. But when springtime came and the tree didn't awaken from its winter slumber, it was time to bring it down.

Every day for a week I worked on that tree—first to fell it and then to chop two decades of growth into manageable pieces. It gave me a lot of time to think about trees.

I thought about the first tree—the one on which hung the forbidden fruit that Adam and Eve just couldn't resist (Genesis 3:6). God used that tree to test their loyalty and trust. Then there's the tree in Psalm 1 that reminds us of the fruitfulness of godly living. And in Proverbs 3:18, wisdom is personified as a tree of life.

But it is a transplanted tree that is most important—the crude cross of Calvary that was hewn from a sturdy tree. There our Savior hung between heaven and earth to bear every sin of every generation on His shoulders. It stands above all trees as a symbol of love, sacrifice, and salvation.

At Calvary, God's only Son suffered a horrible death on a cross. That's the tree of life for us.

—Dave Branon

If I do not have love, I am only a resounding gong.
1 Corinthians 13:1

LOVE LETTER

Read: Psalm 119:97-104

Oh, how I love your law! I meditate on it all day long.
—PSALM 119:97

Each morning when I reach my office, I have one simple habit—check all my emails. Most of the time, I'll work through them in a perfunctory fashion. There are some emails, however, that I'm eager to open. You guessed it—those from loved ones.

Someone has said that the Bible is God's love letter to us. But perhaps on some days, like me, you just don't feel like opening it; and your heart doesn't resonate with the words of the psalmist: "Oh, how I love your law!" (Psalm 119:97). The Scriptures are God's "commands" (v. 98), "statutes" (v. 99), "precepts" (v. 100), and "word" (v. 101).

A question by Thomas Manton (1620–1677), once a lecturer at Westminster Abbey, still holds relevance for us today. He asked: "Who is the author of Scripture? God. . . . What is the end of Scripture? God. Why was the Scripture written, but that we might everlastingly enjoy the blessed God?"

It is said of some people that the more you know them the less you admire them; but the reverse is true of God. Familiarity with the Word of God, or rather the God of the Word, breeds affection, and affection seeks yet greater familiarity.

As you open your Bible, remember that God—the One who loves you the most—has a message for you.

—*Poh Fang Chia*

Love the Lord your God with all your heart and with all your soul and with all your mind and with all your strength.

Mark 12:30

A WONDERFUL EXPLOSION

Read: John 13:31-35

A new command I give you: Love one another. As I have loved you,
so you must love one another. —JOHN 13:34

In the book *Kisses from Katie,* Katie Davis recounts the joy of moving to Uganda and adopting several Ugandan girls. One day, one of her daughters asked, "Mommy, if I let Jesus come into my heart, will I explode?" At first, Katie said no. When Jesus enters our heart, it is a spiritual event.

However, after she thought more about the question, Katie explained that when we decide to give our lives and hearts to Jesus "we will explode with love, with compassion, with hurt for those who are hurting, and with joy for those who rejoice." In essence, knowing Christ results in a deep care for the people in our world.

The Bible challenges us to "rejoice with those who rejoice; mourn with those who mourn" (Romans 12:15). We can consistently display this loving response because of the Holy Spirit's work in our hearts. When we receive Christ, the Holy Spirit comes to live inside us. The apostle Paul described it this way, "When you believed [in Christ,] you were marked in him with a seal, the promised Holy Spirit" (Ephesians 1:13).

Caring for others—with God's supernatural assistance—shows the world that we are His followers (John 13:35). It also reminds us of His love for us. Jesus said, "As I have loved you, so you must love one another" (v. 34).

—*Jennifer Benson Schuldt*

Whoever would love life and see good days must keep their tongue from evil. 1 Peter 3:10

THE GOOD ATHEIST

Read: Luke 10:25-37

The commandments, "You shall not commit adultery,"
"You shall not murder," "You shall not steal," "You shall not covet,"
and whatever other command there may be, are summed up in this one
*command: "Love your neighbor as yourself." —*ROMANS 13:9

When a man learned that an elderly woman could no longer buy her medicine and pay her rent, he came to her rescue. He took her into his home and treated her as if she were his mother. He gave her a bedroom, prepared the food for her meals, bought her medicine, and transported her whenever she needed medical attention. He continued to care for her when she could no longer do much for herself. I was amazed when I learned that this good man was a zealous atheist!

The Jews were shocked by Jesus's parable of the Good Samaritan, because He put him in a positive light. They viewed Samaritans in a negative way — not thinking there was any good in them.

A lawyer had tested Jesus by asking how he could inherit eternal life. Jesus asked him what the law said. The man answered that he must love the Lord with all his heart and his neighbor as himself (Luke 10:25–27). He asked Jesus, "Who is my neighbor?" (v. 29). In Jesus's story, the Samaritan was the neighbor who showed kindness to the wounded man.

Jesus wanted this parable to challenge His listeners. The stories of the Good Samaritan and the good atheist remind us of this high standard of God's Word: "Love your neighbor as yourself" (Romans 13:9).

—Herb Vander Lugt

Love does no harm to a neighbor. Romans 13:10

REAL LOVE

Read: 1 Corinthians 13:1-8

*[Love] always protects, always trusts, always hopes, always perseveres.
Love never fails. But where there are prophecies, they will cease;
where there are tongues, they will be stilled; where there is knowledge,
it will pass away.* —1 CORINTHIANS 13:7–8

A few years ago, my friend's mother was diagnosed with Alzheimer's disease. Since then, Beth has been forced to make tough decisions about her mom's care, and her heart has often been broken as she watched her vibrant and fun-loving mom slowly slipping away. In the process, my friend has learned that real love is not always easy or convenient.

After her mom was hospitalized for a couple of days last year, Beth wrote these words to some of her friends: "As backwards as it may seem, I'm very thankful for the journey I am on with my mom. Behind the memory loss, confusion, and utter helplessness is a beautiful person who loves life and is at complete peace. I am learning so much about what real love is, and even though I probably wouldn't have asked for this journey and the tears and heartache that go with it, I wouldn't trade it for anything."

The Bible reminds us that love is patient and kind. It is not self-seeking or easily angered. It "bears all things, believes all things, hopes all things, endures all things" (1 Corinthians 13:4–7 NKJV).

Real love originated with our Father, who gave us the gift of His Son. As we seek to show His love to others, we can follow the example of Christ, who laid down His life for us (1 John 3:16–18).

—*Cindy Hess Kasper*

Because of his great love for us, God who is rich in mercy, made us alive with Christ. Ephesians 2:4-5

THE REAL THING

Read: 1 John 2:3-11

But if anyone obeys his word, love for God is truly made complete in them.
This is how we know we are in him. —1 JOHN 2:5

A church in Naperville, Illinois, is basking in excitement about its brand-new bells in the belfry above its sanctuary. When the church was built many years ago, the people didn't have the money to purchase bells. However, for its twenty-fifth anniversary they were able to raise the funds to hang three bells in the vacant space. Even though they are stunning, there is one problem: the congregation will never hear the bells ring. Although they look real, they are artificial.

The apostle John wrote his first epistle to encourage believers not to just look like real Christians but also to prove they are genuine by how they live. The evidence that a person's faith is real is not found in some mystical experience with God. The proof that people truly know and love God is found in submitting to His authority and to His Word. John writes, "But if anyone obeys his word, love for God is truly made complete in them. This is how we know we are in him: Whoever claims to live in him must live as Jesus did" (1 John 2:5–6).

If we claim that we have been transformed by the gospel and intimately know and love God, we should validate it by our obedience to His Word.

—Marvin Williams

You, Lord, are forgiving and good. Psalm 86:5

GOATS FOR JESUS

Read: 1 John 3:16-20

If anyone has material possessions and sees a brother or sister in need but has no pity on them, how can the love of God be in that person?
—1 JOHN 3:17

When Dave and Joy Mueller felt God prompting them to move to Sudan as missionaries, all they knew was that they would be helping to build a hospital in that war-ravaged land. How could they know that goats would be in their future?

As Joy began working with the women, she discovered that many were widows because of the devastating civil war and had no way to earn a living. So Joy had an idea. If she could provide just one pregnant goat to a woman, that person would have milk and a source of income. To keep the program going, the woman would give the newborn kid back to Joy—but all other products from the goat would be used to support the woman's family. The baby goat would eventually go to another family. The gift of goats given in Jesus's name would change the life of numerous Sudanese women—and open the door for Joy to explain the gospel.

What is your equivalent to goats? What can you give a neighbor, a friend, or even someone you don't know? Is it a ride? An offer to do yardwork? A gift of material resources?

As believers in Christ, we have the responsibility to care for the needs of others (1 John 3:17). Our acts of love reveal that Jesus resides in our hearts. Giving to those in need may help us tell others about Him.

—*Dave Branon*

Since God so loved us,
we also ought to love one another.

1 John 4:11

⋈

NO OUTSIDERS

Read: Deuteronomy 10:12-22

And now, Israel, what does the LORD your God ask of you but to fear the LORD your God, to walk in obedience to him, to love him, to serve the LORD your God with all your heart and with all your soul.
—DEUTERONOMY 10:12

In the remote region of Ghana where I lived as a boy, "Chop time, no friend" was a common proverb. Locals considered it impolite to visit at "chop time" (mealtime) because food was often scarce. The maxim applied to neighbors and outsiders alike.

But in the Philippines, where I also lived for a time, even if you visit unannounced at mealtime, your hosts will insist on sharing with you regardless of whether they have enough for themselves. Cultures differ for their own good reasons.

As the Israelites left Egypt, God provided specific instructions to govern their culture. But rules—even God's rules—can never change hearts. So Moses said, "Change your hearts and stop being stubborn" (Deuteronomy 10:16 NLT). Interestingly, right after issuing that challenge Moses took up the topic of Israel's treatment of outsiders. God "loves the foreigner residing among you," he said, "giving them food and clothing. And you are to love those who are foreigners, for you yourselves were foreigners in Egypt" (vv. 18–19).

Israel served the "God of gods and Lord of lords, the great God, mighty and awesome" (v. 17). One powerful way they were to show their identification with God was by loving foreigners—those from outside their culture.

What might this small picture of God's character mean for us today? How can we show His love to the marginalized and the needy in our world?

—*Tim Gustafson*

Those whom I love I rebuke and discipline. Revelation 3:19

HUMAN CHESS

Read: 1 John 4:7-12

Dear friends, let us love one another, for love comes from God. Everyone who loves has been born of God and knows God. —1 JOHN 4:7

Chess is an ancient game of strategy. Each player begins with sixteen pieces on the chessboard with the goal of cornering his opponent's king. It has taken different forms over the years. One form is human chess, which was introduced around AD 735 by Charles Martel, Duke of Austrasia. Martel would play the game on giant boards with real people as the pieces. The human pieces were costumed to reflect their status on the board and moved at the whim of the players—manipulating them to their own ends.

Could this human version of the game of chess be one that we sometimes play? We can easily become so driven by our goals that people become just one more pawn we use to achieve them. The Scriptures, however, call us to a different view of those around us. We are to see people as created in the image of God (Genesis 1:26). They are objects of God's love (John 3:16) and deserving of ours as well.

The apostle John wrote, "Dear friends, let us love one another, for love comes from God. Everyone who loves has been born of God and knows God" (1 John 4:7). Because God first loved us, we are to respond by loving Him and the people He created in His image.

—*Bill Crowder*

Anyone who loves me [Jesus] will obey my teaching. John 14:23

LOVING GOD

Read: 1 John 4:7-21

Dear friends, since God so loved us, we also ought to love one another.
—1 JOHN 4:11

Early in our marriage, I thought I knew the ultimate shortcut to my wife's heart. I arrived home one night with a bouquet of a dozen red roses behind my back. When I presented the flowers to Martie, she thanked me graciously, sniffed the flowers, and then took them into the kitchen. Not quite the response I had expected.

It was an introductory lesson in the reality that flowers are not my wife's primary language of love. While she appreciated the gesture, she was mentally calculating the cost of an expensive bouquet of flowers—a budget breaker for a young couple in seminary! And as I've discovered through the years, she is far more interested in my time and attention. When I devote myself to her in an uninterrupted and attentive way, that's when she really feels loved.

Did you ever wonder how God wants us to show that we love Him? We get a clue when we read this note from John: "Anyone who loves God must also love their brother and sister" (1 John 4:21). It's that simple. One of the primary ways we show our love for God is by loving our brothers and sisters in Christ. When we genuinely love each other, it brings pleasure to our heavenly Father.

So watch for opportunities to tell Jesus you love Him. He's infinitely worth whatever it costs.

—*Joe Stowell*

If you keep my commands, you will remain in my love. John 15:10

OVERWHELMING CONCERN

Read: John 13:31-35

"A new command I give you: Love one another. As I have loved you, so you must love one another." —JOHN 13:34

A while ago, I wrote an article about my wife, Marlene, and her struggles with vertigo. When the article appeared, I was unprepared for the tidal wave of response from readers offering encouragement, help, suggestions, and, mostly, concern for her well-being. These messages came from all over the world, from people in all walks of life. Expressions of loving concern for my wife poured in to the point where we could not even begin to answer them all. It was overwhelming in the best kind of way to see the body of Christ respond to Marlene's struggle. We were, and remain, deeply grateful.

At its core, this is how the body is supposed to work. Loving concern for our brothers and sisters in Christ becomes the evidence that we have experienced His love. While addressing the disciples at the Last Supper, Jesus said, "A new command I give to you: Love one another. As I have loved you, so you must love one another. By this everyone will know that you are my disciples" (John 13:34–35).

Marlene and I experienced a sampling of Christlike love and concern in those letters we received. With the help of our Savior and as a way of praising Him, may we show others that kind of love as well.

—Bill Crowder

Anyone who loves God must also love their brother and sister.
1 John 4:21

LOVE THAT WILL NOT LET ME GO

Read: 1 John 4:7-21

Dear friends, since God so loved us, we also ought to love one another.
—1 JOHN 4:11

Love is the centerpiece of thriving relationships. Scripture makes it clear that we need to be people who love—love God with all our hearts, love our neighbor as ourselves, and love our enemies. But it's hard to love when we don't feel loved. Neglected children, spouses who feel ignored by their mates, and parents who are alienated from their children all know the heartache of a life that lacks love.

So, for everyone who longs to be loved, welcome to the pleasure of knowing that you are richly loved by God. Think of the profound impact of His love that was poured out for you at the cross. Meditate on the fact that if you've trusted in Him, His love covers your faults and failures and that you are clothed with His spotless righteousness (Romans 3:22–24). Revel in the fact that nothing can separate you from His love (8:39). Embrace His loving provision of a future secured for you where you will be eternally loved (John 3:16).

When John tells us that we "ought to love one another," he calls us "dear friends" (1 John 4:11). Once you embrace how wonderfully loved you are by God, it will be much easier to be the loving person God calls you to be—even toward those who don't show you love.

—*Joe Stowell*

The earth is full of [God's] unfailing love.

Psalm 33:5

ⴟ

WELL LOVED

Read: 1 John

We love because he first loved us. —1 JOHN 4:19

A friend described his grandmother as one of the greatest influences in his life. Throughout his adult years, he has kept her portrait next to his desk to remind himself of her unconditional love. "I really do believe," he said, "that she helped me learn how to love."

Not everyone has had a similar taste of human love, but through Christ each of us can experience being well loved by God. In 1 John 4, the word *love* occurs twenty-seven times, and in that chapter God's love through Christ is cited as the source of our love for God and for others. "This is love: not that we loved God, but that he loved us and sent his Son as an atoning sacrifice for our sins" (v. 10). "We know and rely on the love God has for us" (v. 16). "We love because he first loved us" (v. 19).

God's love is not a slowly dripping faucet or a well we must dig for ourselves. It is a rushing stream that flows from His heart into ours. Whatever our family background or experiences in life—whether we feel well loved by others or not—we can know love. We can draw from the Lord's inexhaustible source to know His loving care for us, and we can pass that love on to others.

In Christ our Savior, we are well loved.

—*David McCasland*

If you love me, keep my commands. John 14:15

GOD'S LITTLE BLESSINGS

Read: Psalm 36:5-10

How priceless is your unfailing love, O God!
People take refuge in the shadow of your wings. —PSALM 36:7

Our family was at Disney World several years ago when God handed us one of His little blessings. Disney World is a huge place—one hundred and seven acres huge, to be exact. You could walk around for days without seeing someone you know. My wife and I decided to do our own thing while our children sought out the really cool stuff. We parted at 9 a.m. and were planning a rendezvous around 6 p.m.

At about 2 p.m., Sue and I got a craving for tacos. We looked at our map and made our way to a Spanish-sounding place for Mexican food. We had just sat down with our food when we heard, "Hi, Mom. Hi, Dad." Our four amigos had, at the same time, a hankering for a hot burrito.

Ten minutes after they joined us, a violent summer storm ripped through the park with whipping winds, heavy rain, and loud thunder. My wife commented, "I'd be a wreck if the kids weren't with us during this!" It seemed that God had orchestrated our meeting.

Ever notice those blessings from Him? Ever spend time thanking Him for His concern and care? Consider how remarkable it is that the One who created the universe cares enough to intervene in your life. "How priceless is your unfailing love, O God!"

—*Dave Branon*

I live by faith in the Son of God, who loved me and gave himself for me. Galatians 2:20

A MODEST PROPOSAL

Read: Philippians 2:1-11

And being found in appearance as a man, he humbled himself by becoming obedient to death—even death on a cross! —PHILIPPIANS 2:8

As a college student, I heard countless engagement stories. My starry-eyed friends told about glitzy restaurants, mountaintop sunsets, and rides in horse-drawn carriages. I also recall one story about a young man who simply washed his girlfriend's feet. His "modest proposal" proved he understood that humility is vital for a lifelong commitment.

The apostle Paul also understood the significance of humility and how it holds us together. This is especially important in marriage. Paul said to reject "me-first" urges: "Do nothing out of selfish ambition" (Philippians 2:3). Instead, we should value our spouses more than ourselves, and look out for their interests.

Humility in action means serving our spouse, and no act of service is too small or too great. After all, Jesus "humbled himself by becoming obedient to death—even death on a cross!" (v. 8). His selflessness showed His love for us.

What can you do today to humbly serve the one you love? Maybe it's as simple as leaving Brussels sprouts off the dinner menu or as difficult as helping him or her through a long illness. Whatever it is, placing our spouse's needs before our own confirms our commitment to each other through Christlike humility.

—Jennifer Benson Schuldt

He is the faithful God, keeping his covenant of love to a thousand generations. Deuteronomy 7:9

TOUGH TO LOVE

Read: Acts 13:12-23

For about forty years he endured their conduct in the wilderness.
—ACTS 13:18

Years ago I was a camp counselor for some rebellious boys. I found it challenging to deal with their behavior. They would mistreat the animals at the petting zoo and occasionally fight among themselves. So I adopted a calm and firm approach to leading them. And although they often exasperated me, I always made sure their physical needs were taken care of.

Even though I had a kind and loving exterior, I often felt on the inside that I was just "putting up with them." That caused me to prayerfully reflect on how a loving heavenly Father provides for His rebellious children. In telling the story of the Israelites during the exodus, Paul said, "For about forty years [God] endured their conduct in the wilderness" (Acts 13:18). In Greek "endured" most likely means to patiently provide for people's needs despite an ungrateful response.

Some people may not react favorably to our efforts to show care and concern. When this happens, it may help to remember that God is patient with us. And He has given us His Spirit to help us respond with love to those who are hard to love or who are ungrateful (Galatians 5:22–23).

Give us your patience, Lord, for anyone in our lives who is difficult to love.

—*Dennis Fisher*

The LORD loves righteousness and justice. Psalm 33:5

LOVED WELL

Read: Ephesians 3:14-21

I pray that you, being rooted and established in love, may have power, together with all the Lord's holy people, to grasp how wide and long and high and deep is the love of Christ, and to know this love that surpasses knowledge—that you may be filled to the measure of all the fullness of God. —EPHESIANS 3:17–19

We were gathered with family for Thanksgiving dinner when someone asked if each person would share what he or she was thankful for. One by one we talked. Three-year-old Joshua was thankful for "music," and Nathan, aged four, for "horses." We were all silenced, though, when Stephen (who was soon to turn five) answered, "I'm thankful that Jesus loves me so well." In his simple faith, he understood and was grateful for the love of Jesus for him personally. He told us that Jesus showed His love by dying on a cross.

The apostle Paul wanted the believers in the church at Ephesus to understand how well God loved them, and that was his prayer: That they would be able "to grasp how wide and long and high and deep is the love of Christ" (Ephesians 3:17–19). He prayed that they would be rooted and grounded in that love.

To ground ourselves in God's love, it would be helpful to review these verses frequently—or even memorize them. We can also take a few minutes each day to thank the Lord for the specific ways He shows His love to us. This will help us to grow in our belief and be thankful—as Stephen is—that Jesus loves us "so well."

—Anne Cetas

Let no debt remain outstanding, except the continuing debt to love one another.
Romans 13:8

)X(

HELPFUL LOVE

Read: John 1:9-14

The Word became flesh and made his dwelling among us. We have seen his glory, the glory of the one and only Son, who came from the Father, full of grace and truth. —JOHN 1:14

At the end of my mother's earthly journey, she and Dad were still very much in love and shared a strong faith in Christ. My mother had developed dementia and began to lose memories of even her family. Yet Dad would regularly visit her at the assisted living home and find ways to accommodate her diminished capacities.

For instance, he would take her some saltwater taffy, unwrap a piece, and place it in her mouth—something she could not do for herself. Then as she slowly chewed the candy, Dad would quietly sit with her and hold her hand. When their time together was over, Dad, beaming with a wide smile, would say, "I feel such peace and joy spending time with her."

Though touched by Dad's great joy in helping Mom, I was more affected by the reality that he was depicting God's grace. Jesus was willing to humble himself to connect with us in our weaknesses. In reflecting on Christ's incarnation, John wrote, "The Word became flesh and made his dwelling among us" (1:14). Taking on human limitations, He did countless acts of compassion to accommodate us in our weakness.

Do you know anyone who might benefit from Jesus's helpful, accommodating love that could flow through you to them today?

—*Dennis Fisher*

Be devoted to one another in love. Honor one another above yourselves. Romans 12:10

THE REAL PRIZE

Read: Ephesians 5:22-33

Husbands, love your wives, just as Christ loved the church and gave himself up for her. —EPHESIANS 5:25

I've been amazed at the impact that my wife, Martie, has had on the lives of our kids. Very few roles demand the kind of unconditional, self-sacrificing perseverance and commitment as that of motherhood. I know for certain that my character and faith have been shaped and molded by my mom, Corabelle. Let's face it, where would we be without our wives and mothers?

It reminds me of one of my favorite memories in sports history. Phil Mickelson walked up the eighteenth fairway at the Masters Golf Tournament in 2010 after his final putt to clinch one of golf's most coveted prizes for the third time. But it wasn't his victory leap on the green that had an impact on me. It was when he made a beeline through the crowd to his wife, who was battling life-threatening cancer. They embraced, and the camera caught a tear running down Phil's cheek as he held his wife close for a long time.

Our wives need to experience the kind of sacrificial, selfless love that has been shown to us by the Lover of our souls. As Paul put it, "Husbands, love your wives, just as Christ loved the church and gave himself up for her" (Ephesians 5:25). Prizes come and go, but it's the people you love—and who love you—that matter most.

—*Joe Stowell*

———

Love each other as I have loved you. John 15:12

MORE AND MORE!

Read: 1 Thessalonians 3:12–4:10

May the Lord make your love increase and overflow for each other and for everyone else, just as ours does for you. —1 THESSALONIANS 3:12

A rallying cry often heard today in our economically challenged world is "Less and less." Governments are called to balance their budgets. People are urged to use less energy and decrease consumption of limited resources. It is good advice that we should all heed. In the realm of faith, however, there are no shortages of love and grace and strength. Therefore, as followers of Christ, we are urged to demonstrate His love in our lives in ever-increasing measure.

In the apostle Paul's first letter to the believers in Thessalonica, he urged them to live in a lifestyle that pleases God and to do this "more and more" (4:1). He also commended them for their demonstration of love for each other, and called them to love "more and more" (v. 10).

That kind of ever-increasing love is possible only because it comes from God's limitless resources, not from our own dwindling supply. Poet Annie Johnson Flint wrote:

His love has no limit, His grace has no measure,

His power has no boundary known unto men;

For out of His infinite riches in Jesus,

He giveth, and giveth, and giveth again.

The apostle Paul expressed his desire for the believers: "May the Lord make your love increase and overflow for each other and for everyone else, just as ours does for you" (1 Thessalonians 3:12).

How much should we love God and others? More and more!

—*David McCasland*

Bear with one another in love. Ephesians 4:2

A LOVING FATHER

Read: Psalm 103:7-13

As a father has compassion on his children, so the LORD has compassion on those who fear him. —PSALM 103:13

The parents were obviously weary from dragging their two energetic preschoolers through airports and airplanes, and now their final flight was delayed. As I watched the two boys running around the crowded gate area, I wondered how Mom and Dad were going to keep the little guys settled down for our half-hour flight into Grand Rapids. When we finally boarded, I noticed that the father and one of the sons were in the seats behind me. Then I heard the weary father say to his son, "Why don't you let me read one of your storybooks to you." During the entire flight, this loving father softly and patiently read to his son, keeping him calm and focused.

In one of his psalms David declares, "As a father has compassion on his children, so the LORD has compassion on those who fear him" (Psalm 103:13). This tender word *compassion* gives us a picture of how deeply our heavenly Father loves His children, and it reminds us what a great gift it is to be able to look to God and cry, "Abba, Father" (Romans 8:15).

God longs for you to listen again to the story of His love for you when you are restless on your own journey through life. Your heavenly Father is always near, ready to encourage you with His Word.

—Bill Crowder

We know that in all things God works for the good of those who love him. Romans 8:28

BECAUSE I LOVE HIM

Read: Revelation 22:12-21

He who testifies to these things says, "Yes, I am coming soon."
Amen. Come, Lord Jesus. —REVELATION 22:20

The day before my husband was to return home from a business trip, my son said, "Mom! I want Daddy to come home." I asked him why, expecting him to say something about the presents his daddy usually brings back or that he missed playing ball with him. But with solemn seriousness he answered, "I want him to come back because I love him!"

His answer made me think about our Lord and His promise to come back. "I am coming soon," Jesus says (Revelation 22:20). I long for His return, but why do I want Him to come back? Is it because I will be in His presence, away from sickness and death? Is it because I am tired of living in a difficult world? Or is it because when you've loved Him so much of your life, when He has shared your tears and your laughter, when He has been more real than anybody else, you want to be with Him forever?

I'm glad my son misses his daddy when he's away. It would be terrible if he didn't care at all about his return or if he thought it would interfere with his plans. How do we feel about our Lord's return? Let us long for that day passionately, and earnestly say, "Lord, come back! We love you."

—*Keila Ochoa*

What great love the Father has lavished on us, that we should be called children of God!

1 John 3:1

WHERE HAS THE LOVE GONE?

Read: Jeremiah 2:1-13

This is what the LORD says: "What fault did your ancestors find in me, that they strayed so far from me? They followed worthless idols and became worthless themselves." —JEREMIAH 2:5

New love is exciting! We've all seen it in newly married couples. It doesn't matter if they're twenty or seventy, love makes their faces beautiful and their feet bounce.

It's not only true of marriages. We've seen people who lovingly wash and wax their new sports car—and then do it all over again.

Whether it's a new car or a new relationship, at first we respond with wholehearted devotion. But with the passing of time excitement often fades. Unrealistic hopes can blind us to the flaws in the object of our affection. When we expect too much from a person or a possession, we set ourselves up for disappointment.

A car, a house, or a spouse may turn out to be less than ideal. But if our relationship with God cools, it's because our communication has broken down and disinterest has set in. It's then that intimacy is lost. It happened with Israel (Jeremiah 2:5–8); it happens with us. But we can't blame God. He never changes. His love for us is unfailing!

If your relationship with the Lord has grown cold, take time to think about who He is and what He has done. Draw close to Him again in prayer. Then you won't be left wondering where your love has gone.

—*Mart DeHaan*

——

You are to love those who are foreigners. Deuteronomy 10:19

PURE LOVE

Read: 1 Corinthians 6:18-7:9

But if they cannot control themselves, they should marry, for it is better to marry than to burn with passion. —1 CORINTHIANS 7:9

A situation that once was viewed by most people as unacceptable and immoral has become commonplace. According to the *National & International Religion Report,* before the majority of American marriages take place, the man and woman have already been living together.

The report goes on to point out that this practice has devastating effects. "Marriages that are preceded by living together have fifty percent higher disruption (divorce or separation) rates than marriages without premarital cohabitation."

Even among Christians there is no shortage of those who think they can violate God's moral standards.

The temptations were similar in the first century. That's why Paul had to make it clear to the believers at Corinth that they had no business being involved in sexual immorality. He said that if they found their passions becoming so strong that they could not control their sexual desires, there was an answer. It was not found in an immoral relationship; it was found in marriage.

In a day when immorality continues to devour people, let's do all we can to promote the joys and privileges of love that is honoring to God—the love that is shared in marriage. There is no substitute for pure love.

—*Dave Branon*

Each of you must love his wife as he loves himself. Ephesians 5:33

HIS UNFAILING LOVE

Read: Romans 8:31-39

For I am convinced that neither death nor life, neither angels nor demons, neither the present nor the future, nor any powers, neither height nor depth, nor anything else in all creation, will be able to separate us from the love of God that is in Christ Jesus our Lord. —ROMANS 8:38–39

When Gillian learned one Saturday morning that her daughter had been killed, she was plunged into despair. For eighteen months she pleaded with God for help in her grief. "I've been told that God is love. Why won't He show me His love?" she told me.

Then, a little while later, Gillian experienced what she refers to as "a small miracle—a tiny glow of warmth deep in my soul, which grew to an all-consuming love—the love of Jesus." "Dear Jesus," she said, "my search to find you has led me down many paths, but when the right time came you showed me the way."

Gillian's search for love ended when she found Christ as her Savior, but her need for Him had only begun. A few months later, her twenty-year-long marriage ended in divorce because of her husband's unfaithfulness. "I've failed many times," she said, "but I know God's love for me is real, and I hold on to the knowledge that I am loved by Him."

The apostle Paul came to know God's love on the road to Damascus (Acts 9). Over the years he too found it to be unfailing. Nothing else could account for the amazing words he penned in Romans 8:38–39.

Are you searching for God's unfailing love? It's available if you will seek Him with all your heart.

—*Dennis DeHaan*

Many waters cannot quench love; rivers cannot sweep it away.
Song of Solomon 8:7

THE RIGHT TRIANGLE

Read: Colossians 3:16-24

And whatever you do, whether in word or deed, do it all in the name
of the Lord Jesus, giving thanks to God the Father through him.
—COLOSSIANS 3:17

Although we usually think of a marriage triangle as a danger-ous situation, there is one sense in which a third person could create the right triangle.

Viola Walden tells the story of a newly married couple riding a train on their honeymoon. A silver-haired man leaned across the aisle and asked, "Is there a third party going with you on your honeymoon?" The couple looked at him strangely; then he added, "When Sarah and I were married, we invited Jesus to our marriage. One of the first things we did in our new home was to kneel and ask Jesus to make our marriage a love triangle—Sarah, myself, and Jesus. And all three of us have been in love with each other for all fifty years of our married life."

When the Lord Jesus is invited into a marriage to stay, His love fills both heart and home. Notice that before Paul gave instructions to husbands and wives in Colossians 3, he said to do "all in the name of the Lord Jesus." If a couple lives by that principle when difficult times come, Jesus is there to mediate the disagreement. When tough decisions must be made, He is wisdom. When the home experiences grief, He stands by to comfort and cheer. And He is the One who brings genuine happiness.

When a husband and wife are in love with each other and with Jesus, they form the right triangle.

—*Paul Van Gorder*

Keep your lives free from the love of money. Hebrews 13:5

FOR HUSBANDS ONLY

Read: Ephesians 5:25-33

Husbands, love your wives, just as Christ loved the church and gave himself up for her. —EPHESIANS 5:25

If a husband would love his wife as much as Christ loved the church, what a tremendous difference it would make in their marriage! Such sacrificial love would put an end to all rude, inconsiderate behavior on the husband's part. He would be kind, caring, and forgiving. He would be far more concerned about his wife's happiness than his own well-being. In fact, he would even be willing to die for her.

A man was telling Pastor Rowland Hill of London about the death of another pastor's wife. He commented that the Lord must have taken her because the man loved her too much. Upon hearing that, Hill bristled and exclaimed, "What? Can a man love his wife too much? Impossible! Unless he could love her better than Christ loves the church."

In Ephesians 5:25, the apostle Paul commanded, "Husbands, love your wives, just as Christ loved the church and gave himself up for her." And in Colossians 3:19, he said, "Husbands, love your wives and do not be harsh with them." If a husband loves his wife with Christlike love, it is impossible to love her too much!

In view of our Lord's great example of love for us, we should seek to pattern our lives after Him. A husband need never be concerned about loving his wife too much. Instead, he should frequently ask himself, "Do I love her enough?"

—*Richard DeHaan*

Let us consider how we may spur one another on toward love and good deeds.

Hebrews 10:24

THE BEAUTIFUL BRIDE

Read: Revelation 19:4-9

Let us rejoice and be glad and give him glory! For the wedding of the Lamb has come, and his bride has made herself ready.
—REVELATION 19:7

I have officiated many weddings. Often planned according to the dreams of the bride, each of the weddings has been unique. But one thing is the same: adorned in their wedding dresses with hair beautifully done and faces aglow, brides steal the show.

I find it intriguing that God describes us as His bride. Speaking of the church, He says, "The marriage of the Lamb has come, and his Bride has made herself ready" (Revelation 19:7 ESV).

This is a great thought for those of us who have become discouraged about the condition of the church. I grew up as a pastor's kid, pastored three churches, and have preached in churches all over the world. I've counseled both pastors and parishioners about deep and troubling problems in the church. And though the church often seems unlovable, my love for the church has not changed.

But my reason for loving the church has changed. I now love it most of all for whose it is. The church belongs to Christ; it is the bride of Christ. Since the church is precious to Him, it is precious to me as well. His love for His bride, as flawed as we may be, is nothing less than extraordinary!

—*Joe Stowell*

"Simon, do you love me?" "Feed my lambs." John 21:15

"I DON'T EVEN LIKE HER"

Read John 13:31-35

A new command I give you: Love one another. As I have loved you,
so you must love one another. —JOHN 13:34

When Missy started her new job in the factory, she was determined to let her light shine for the Lord. But as soon as she met Louise, her work partner, she knew it wasn't going to be easy. Brassy, defensive, and crude, Louise ridiculed everything Missy did. When Missy tried to befriend her and tell her about Jesus, she was rejected. Louise said, "I tried that. It didn't work."

Missy asked God for help. She opened her Bible to John 13:34, "A new command I give you: Love one another. As I have loved you, so you must love one another." So Missy kept trying to show love. But all she met was hardness.

After a particularly rough day at work, Missy opened her Bible and cried out to God. Again, her eyes fell on John 13:34. "But I don't even like her!" Missy complained.

One day Louise sat beside Missy at break and said, "You're the only person who cares." Then she poured out a story of heartache and trouble. Missy put her arms around her, and they became friends. Louise attended church with Missy and, after a struggle, opened her heart to Jesus.

This true story has a happy ending, but not all do. Even so, as faithful followers of Jesus, we are to let His light shine brightly through our love.

—*David Egner*

To godliness, mutual affection; and to mutual affection, love.
2 Peter 1:7

LOVING IS DOING

Read: Luke 10:30-37

Let no debt remain outstanding, except the continuing debt to love one another. —ROMANS 13:8

The eminent psychologist Erich Fromm said that love is "an action, not a passion." This is borne out in Christian experience. For instance, we may say we love our wife, our husband, our sweetheart, or our neighbor, but if that love is indeed real, our actions will demonstrate it.

In his book *Mere Christianity*, C. S. Lewis wrote, "Do not waste your time bothering whether you 'love' your neighbor; act as if you did. As soon as we do this, we find one of the great secrets. When you are behaving as if you loved someone, you will presently come to love him. If you injure someone you dislike, you will find yourself disliking him more. If you do him a good turn, you will find yourself disliking him less."

When I was a student in a Bible institute, one of the young men living in our dorm was a guy I just didn't like. I thought he was arrogant. He had few friends. One night after an intramural basketball game, that unpopular student and I happened to walk back to the dorm together. I tried my best to show him Christian friendship; in fact, I took him to the Sweet Shop and bought him a milkshake. As we talked, he told me of his father's serious illness and his family's poverty. I began to appreciate this misunderstood dorm mate. Years later I learned that just before that night he had been ready to quit school. Today he is a successful pastor.

Loving is doing. Jesus demonstrated that when He died for us. Is there someone to whom you should show love?

—*David Egner*

We rely on the love God has for us. 1 John 4:16

REALISM AND ROMANCE

Read: Ephesians 5:22-33

Husbands, love your wives, just as Christ loved the church and gave himself up for her. However, each one of you also must love his wife as he loves himself, and the wife must respect her husband.
—EPHESIANS 5:25, 33

Good marriages have a balance. The practical realities of daily living are enhanced by the joy and spontaneity of continually falling in love with each other.

Realism can help a husband to see that he is taking his wife for granted and is not being sensitive to her feelings. It can cause a wife to see that her critical comments are tearing down her husband's self-respect.

Realism is not enough, however. Romance, often discarded after the wedding, keeps a marriage from growing dull. It can prevent the kind of situation depicted in the cartoon of an elderly couple sitting on the front porch of their home. The husband is saying, "Sometimes, Sarah, when I think of how much you mean to me, I can hardly keep from telling you so."

Paul's words in Ephesians 5 encourage a love between two people that reflects Christ's self-sacrificing devotion to His church. In addition, it's a love filled with kindness and tenderness.

Whether you've have been married half a year or half a century, Christ can help you balance your relationship with realism and romance. Keep drawing on His love and see what it does for your marriage.

—*Dennis DeHaan*

God's love has been poured out in our hearts through the Holy Spirit. Romans 5:5

THE POWER OF LOVE

Read: 1 John 4:7-10

This is love: not that we loved God, but that he loved us and sent his Son as an atoning sacrifice for our sins. —1 JOHN 4:10

Books on leadership often appear on bestseller lists. Most of them tell how to become a powerful and effective leader. But Henri Nouwen's book *In the Name of Jesus: Reflections on Christian Leadership* is written from a different perspective. The former university professor who spent many years serving in a community of developmentally disabled adults says: "The question is not: How many people take you seriously? How much are you going to accomplish? Can you show some results? But: Are you in love with Jesus? . . . In our world of loneliness and despair, there is an enormous need for men and women who know the heart of God, a heart that forgives, that cares, that reaches out and wants to heal."

John wrote, "This is how God showed his love among us: He sent his one and only Son into the world that we might live through him. This is love: not that we loved God, but that he loved us and sent his Son as an atoning sacrifice for our sins" (1 John 4:9–10).

"The Christian leader of the future," writes Nouwen, "is the one who truly knows the heart of God as it has become flesh . . . in Jesus." In Him, we discover and experience God's unconditional, unlimited love.

—*David McCasland*

Love one another deeply, from the heart.

1 Peter 1:22

⋊⋉

NO GREATER LOVE

Read: 1 John 4:7-11

Dear friends, since God so loved us, we also ought to love one another.
—1 JOHN 4:11

On our family-room wall, in a small shadowbox, hangs a "treasure" that belongs to my wife Carolyn. Oh, we have things more intrinsically valuable on the walls of our home—a handmade quilt from the Blue Ridge Mountains of Kentucky, antique mirrors, oil paintings, and a magnificent dulcimer from an artisan in the backcountry of Idaho.

Carolyn's treasure, though, is far more valuable to her than any other possession, for it contains a gift from our granddaughter Julia. It was a present to her "Nana" on Valentine's Day several years ago when Julia was only six years old—a small, red, clay heart. Inscribed on it in childish scrawl are the words "I Luv U."

The little heart is crudely made, ragged on the edges, and bears a number of thumbprints and smudges, but Carolyn has enshrined it in a frame made especially for that heart. Each day it reminds her of Julia's love.

Is God's love more valuable to you than silver or gold or any other possession? He "sent his one and only Son into the world that [you] might live through him" (1 John 4:9). He did that because He loves you—not because you loved Him. And because of His love, one day you will be with Him in heaven. There is no greater love!

—*David Roper*

The only thing that counts is faith expressing itself through love.
Galatians 5:6

NO WONDER!

Read: Song of Solomon 1:1-4

We love Him because He first loved us. —1 JOHN 4:19 NKJV

"He's perfect for you," my friend told me. She was talking about a guy she had just met. She described his kind eyes, his kind smile, and his kind heart. When I met him I had to agree. Today he's my husband, and no wonder I love him!

In the Song of Solomon the bride describes her lover. His love is better than wine and more fragrant than ointments. His name is sweeter than anything in this world. So she concludes that it's no wonder he is loved.

But there is Someone far greater than any earthly loved one, Someone whose love is also better than wine. His love satisfies our every need. His "fragrance" is better than any perfume because when He gave himself for us; His sacrifice became a sweet-smelling aroma to God (Ephesians 5:2). Finally, His name is above every name (Philippians 2:9). No wonder we love Him!

It is a privilege to love Jesus. It is the best experience in life! Do we take the time to tell Him so? Do we express with words the beauty of our Savior? If we show His beauty with our lives, others will say, "No wonder you love Him!"

—*Keila Ochoa*

—————

Christ's love compels us. 2 Corinthians 5:14

AMBASSADOR OF LOVE

Read: John 3:9-21

For God did not send his Son into the world to condemn the world,
but to save the world through him. —JOHN 3:17

In my work as a chaplain, some people occasionally ask if I am willing to give them some additional spiritual help. While I'm happy to spend time with anyone who asks for help, I often find myself doing more learning than teaching. This was especially true when one painfully honest new Christian said to me with resignation, "I don't think it's a good idea for me to read the Bible. The more I read what God expects from me, the more I judge others who aren't doing what it says."

As he said this, I realized that I was at least partly responsible for instilling this judgmental spirit in him. At that time, one of the first things I did with those new to faith in Jesus was to introduce them to things they should no longer be doing. In other words, instead of showing them God's love and letting the Holy Spirit reshape them, I urged them to "behave like a believer."

Now I was gaining a new appreciation for John 3:16–17. Jesus's invitation to believe in Him in verse 16 is followed by these words. "For God did not send his Son into the world to condemn the world, but to save the world through him."

Jesus didn't come to condemn us. But by giving these new Christians a checklist of behaviors, I was teaching them to condemn themselves, which then led them to judge others. Instead of being agents of condemnation, we are to be ambassadors of God's love and mercy.

—*Randy Kilgore*

Love does not boast. 1 Corinthians 13:4

THE FORGOTTEN WORKER

Read: Hebrews 6:9–20

*God is not unjust; he will not forget your work and the love you have
shown him as you have helped his people and continue to help them.*
—HEBREWS 6:10

People around the world are familiar with Mount Rushmore,
the South Dakota site where the heads of former American
presidents are carved in gigantic scale on a cliff wall. Yet,
while millions know of Mount Rushmore, relatively few know
the name Doane Robinson—the South Dakota state historian
who conceived the idea of the magnificent sculpture and man-
aged the project. The monument is admired and appreciated,
but he is the forgotten man behind the masterpiece. His name
is largely unrecognized or was never even known by some.

Sometimes, in the service of the Master, we may feel that
we have been forgotten or are behind the scenes and not rec-
ognized. Ministry can be a life of effort that often goes unap-
preciated by the very people we are seeking to serve in Jesus's
name. The good news, however, is that, while people may not
know, God does. Hebrews 6:10 says, "For God is not unjust
to forget your work and labor of love which you have shown
toward His name, in that you have ministered to the saints,
and do minister" (NKJV).

What a promise! Our heavenly Father will never forget our
service to Him and our labor of love. That is infinitely more
important than being applauded by the crowds.

—*Bill Crowder*

**Great is [God's] love, reaching to the heavens; your faithfulness
reaches to the skies. Psalm 57:10**

STOP TO HELP

Read: Luke 10:30-37

"'Love the Lord your God with all your heart and with all your soul and with all your strength and with all your mind'; and, 'Love your neighbor as yourself.' " —LUKE 10:27

Dr. Scott Kurtzman, chief of surgery at Waterbury Hospital in Connecticut, was on his way to deliver a lecture when he witnessed a horrible crash involving twenty vehicles. The doctor shifted into trauma mode, worked his way through the mess of metal, and called out, "Who needs help?" After ninety minutes of assisting, and the victims were taken to area hospitals, Dr. Kurtzman commented, "A person with my skills simply can't drive by someone who is injured. I refuse to live my life that way."

Jesus told a parable about a man who stopped to help another (Luke 10:30–37). A Jewish man had been ambushed, stripped, robbed, and left for dead. A Jewish priest and a temple assistant passed by, saw the man, and crossed over to the other side. Then a despised Samaritan came by, saw the man, and was filled with compassion. His compassion was translated into action: He soothed and bandaged the man's wounds, took him to an inn, cared for him while he could, paid for all his medical expenses, and then promised the innkeeper he would return to pay any additional expenses.

There are people around us who are suffering. Moved with compassion for their pain, let's be those who stop to help.

—*Marvin Williams*

The goal . . . is love, which comes from a pure heart and a good conscience and a sincere faith.

1 Timothy 1:5

✕

GUARD YOUR BRAND

Read: Colossians 3:1-14

And over all these virtues put on love, which binds them all together in perfect unity. —COLOSSIANS 3:14

A popular clothing retailer requires that its sales clerks dress like the models in the store windows, which advertise its clothes. This practice is referred to as "guarding their brand." The idea behind it is that shoppers will be more likely to purchase clothes because they will want to look like the people they see wearing them.

In a consumer-oriented culture, it's easy to be seduced into thinking that we can "buy" acceptance by wearing the things that beautiful people wear. Retailers would have us believe that looking good will make us desirable.

Sometimes we even convince ourselves that we can win followers for God by making ourselves attractive to the world. But the Bible is clear about what's really important to God. He wants us to look like Jesus in our character. In a sense, Jesus is our "brand," for we are being conformed to His image (Romans 8:29). We attract others to Christ when we put on His attributes, which include compassion, kindness, humility, gentleness, patience (Colossians 3:12), and, above all, love (v. 14).

Instead of polishing and protecting our own image, we need to be guarding and reflecting the image of God, which is being perfected in us through Christ.

—*Julie Ackerman Link*

———

Neither death nor life, neither angels nor demons, neither the present nor the future, nor any powers, neither height nor depth, nor anything else in all creation, will be able to separate us from the love of God that is in Christ Jesus our Lord. Romans 8:38-39

OUR DAILY BREAD WRITERS

JAMES BANKS

Pastor of Peace Church in Durham, North Carolina, Dr. James Banks has written several books for Discovery House, including *Praying Together* and *Prayers for Prodigals*.

DAVE BRANON

An editor with Discovery House, Dave has been involved with *Our Daily Bread* since the 1980s. He has written several books, including *Beyond the Valley* and *Stand Firm*, both DH publications.

ANNE CETAS

After becoming a Christian in her late teens, Anne was introduced to *Our Daily Bread* right away and began reading it. Now she reads it for a living as the managing editor of *Our Daily Bread*.

POH FANG CHIA

Like Anne Cetas, Poh Fang trusted Jesus Christ as Savior as a teenager. She is an editor and a part of the Chinese editorial review committee serving in the Our Daily Bread Ministries Singapore office.

BILL CROWDER

A former pastor who is now an associate teacher for Our Daily Bread Ministries, Bill travels extensively as a Bible conference teacher, sharing God's truths with fellow believers in Malaysia and Singapore and other places where ODB Ministries has international offices. His Discovery House books include *Windows on Easter* and *Let's Talk*.

DENNIS DEHAAN

When Henry Bosch retired, Dennis became the second managing editor of *Our Daily Bread*. A former pastor, he loved preaching and teaching the Word of God. Dennis went to be with the Lord in 2014.

MART DEHAAN

The former president of Our Daily Bread Ministries, Mart followed in the footsteps of his grandfather M. R. and his dad Richard in that capacity. Mart, who has long been associated with *Day of Discovery* as host of the program from Israel, is now senior content advisor for Our Daily Bread Ministries.

RICHARD DEHAAN

Son of the founder of Our Daily Bread Ministries, Dr. M. R. DeHaan, Richard was responsible for the ministry's entrance into television. Under his leadership, *Day of Discovery* television made its debut in 1968.

DAVID EGNER

A retired Our Daily Bread Ministries editor and longtime *Our Daily Bread* writer, David was also a college professor during his working career. In fact, he was a writing instructor for both Anne Cetas and Julie Ackerman Link at Cornerstone University.

DENNIS FISHER

As a senior research editor at Our Daily Bread Ministries, Dennis uses his theological training to guarantee biblical accuracy. He is also an expert in C. S. Lewis studies.

VERNON GROUNDS

A longtime college president (Denver Seminary) and board member for Our Daily Bread Ministries, Vernon's life story was told in the Discovery House book *Transformed by Love*. Dr. Grounds died in 2010 at the age of 96.

TIM GUSTAFSON

Tim writes for *Our Daily Bread* and *Our Daily Journey* and serves as an editor for Discovery Series. As the son of missionaries to Ghana, Tim has an unusual perspective on life in the West. He and his wife, Leisa, are the parents of one daughter and seven sons.

CINDY HESS KASPER

An editor for the Our Daily Bread Ministries publication *Our Daily Journey*, Cindy began writing for *Our Daily Bread* in 2006. She and her husband, Tom, have three children and seven grandchildren.

RANDY KILGORE

Randy spent most of his 20-plus years in business as a senior human resource manager before returning to seminary. Since finishing his Masters in Divinity in 2000, he has served as a writer and workplace chaplain. A collection of those devotionals appears in the Discovery House book, *Made to Matter: Devotions for Working Christians*. Randy and his wife, Cheryl, and their two children live in Massachusetts.

JULIE ACKERMAN LINK

A book editor by profession, Julie began writing for *Our Daily Bread* in 2000. Her books *Above All, Love* and *A Heart for God* are available through Discovery House. Julie lost her long battle with cancer in April 2015.

DAVID MCCASLAND

Living in Colorado, David enjoys the beauty of God's grandeur as displayed in the Rocky Mountains. An accomplished biographer, David has written several books, including the award-winning *Oswald Chambers: Abandoned to God,* and *Eric Liddell: Pure Gold.*

KEILA OCHOA

From her home in Mexico, Keila assists with Media Associates International, a group that trains writers around the world to write about faith. She and her husband have two young children.

DAVID ROPER

David Roper lives in Idaho, where he takes advantage of the natural beauty of his state. He has been writing for *Our Daily Bread* since 2000, and he has published several successful books with Discovery House, including *Out of the Ordinary* and *Teach Us To Number Our Days.*

JENNIFER BENSON SCHULDT

Chicagoan Jennifer Schuldt writes from the perspective of a mom of a growing family. She has written for *Our Daily Bread* since 2010, and she also pens articles for another Our Daily Bread Ministries publication: *Our Daily Journey.*

JOE STOWELL

As president of Cornerstone University, Joe stays connected to today's young adults in a leadership role. A popular speaker and a former pastor, Joe has written a number of books over the years, including *Strength for the Journey* and *Jesus Nation*.

MARION STROUD

After a battle with cancer, Marion went to be with her Savior in August 2015. Marion began writing devotional articles for *Our Daily Bread* in 2014. Two of her popular books of prayers, *Dear God, It's Me and It's Urgent* and *It's Just You and Me, Lord* were published by Discovery House.

HERB VANDER LUGT

For many years, Herb was senior research editor at Our Daily Bread Ministries, responsible for checking the biblical accuracy of the booklets published by ODB Ministries. A World War II veteran, Herb spent several years as a pastor before his ODB tenure began. Herb went to be with his Lord and Savior in 2006.

MARVIN WILLIAMS

Marvin's first foray into Our Daily Bread Ministries came as a writer for *Our Daily Journey*. In 2007, he penned his first *Our Daily Bread* article. Marvin is senior teaching pastor at a church in Lansing, Michigan.

SCRIPTURE INDEX
OF KEY VERSES

NOTE TO THE READER

The publisher invites you to share your response to the message of this book by writing Discovery House, P.O. Box 3566, Grand Rapids, MI 49501, USA. For information about other Discovery House books, music, or DVDs, contact us at the same address or call 1-800-653-8333. Find us online at dhp.org or send e-mail to books@dhp.org.